GOOD LOOKIN' MAN LIKE ME

A Luminous Portrait of a Life That Transcends Constraints

by LYLE JACOBSON

ISBN: 0615492959
ISBN-13: 9780615492957
Library of Congress Control Number: 2011908879

DEDICATION

To Mom and Dad, whose faith, love and example gave each of us "Jacobson boys" a zest for life, a love for people and for each other, and the personal confidence to meet any hardship without fear.

ACKNOWLEDGEMENTS

A special thanks goes to my brother and best friend, Ralph Jacobson, who has been a constant source of fun and companionship my entire life. His recollection of events in Wendy's life and insights into Wendy's personality provided much of the material used for this book. Rich Buhler gave me the initial impetus to document the story of our family, and has provided much encouragement and direction for writing this account of my brother's life. Karen Todd, a retired English teacher helped me with grammar, spelling and syntax. Sherri Powers, a college classmate and long-time friend, and my sister-in-law, Donna Jacobson helped immensely by proof-reading the initial copy of the book. My wife and sweetheart, Diann, spurred me on to complete the book with unequivocal praise, support and patience.

To the loving people in our extended family, church friends and neighbors, staffers in the social services industry and the many sensitive "strangers" who have cared for and enjoyed Wendy, I say, "Thank you" and "Bless you." You have helped my brother to see himself as a "good lookin' man."

FORWARD

Wendy Jacobson was my first introduction to a developmentally disabled person who had been mainstreamed as much as possible by his family. I was in college at the time and his brother, Lyle Jacobson, had been a roommate and a good friend.

I met Wendy one summer when I was visiting in Sacramento where the Jacobsons lived. Like many others I was ignorant about people like Wendy and confess to being uncomfortable with their disabilities. But Wendy was different. He was fun-loving, funny, and a delight to be with. It didn't take me long to look past his physical and mental challenges and see a precious and unique person whom I looked forward to seeing the next time.

Wendy was a young adult at the time and had developed a reputation for riding his bicycle to the local shopping center and making the rounds of all the people he had befriended there ranging from clerks to business owners.

I was most fascinated, however, by watching him and his family interact. That was the secret to Wendy's success. He was not shuffled to the sidelines. He was as much a member of the family as any of the others and that investment in Wendy's life became apparent the more I got to know him. He was just one of the guys and took as much ribbing as any of them and laughed his way through it.

That was more than 40 years ago and Wendy remains one of my favorite people. We had the privilege last year of attending his 70th birthday in Sacramento and it was a testimony to Wendy's life. There must have been 50 people there and I wondered during the party how many other people like Wendy had accumulated such a roster of friends.

He's very special and I'm thankful to be counted among his friends.

I have to give tribute to his brother Lyle who has remained faithful to Wendy on a daily basis, sustained all the good things that have been deposited in Wendy's life, and who has captured in writing so many wonderful "Wendy Moments" for us all to enjoy.

Rich Buhler, Author, Broadcaster, Speaker

CONTENTS

A Special Brother 1

Damaged Goods 5

Bad to the Bone 13

Automania 19

The Miracle 23

Girls, Girls, Girls 29

Cigawrecks 35

Doctor Dread 41

The Disability "Hat Trick" 45

Death, Where is Thy Sting? 49

Friends High and Low 55

We Are Family 59

Sunday-Go-to-Meetin' 65

Dogs and Forgiveness 69

Good Lookin' Man Like Me 73

A Blinded Eye 77

Stuck 81

Never Look Back. 85

Staff Affection 89

A Child Forever. 95

Jake and Neva 101

You Look Like Your Brother 107

Epilogue 113

A SPECIAL BROTHER

It was sometime later in our lives that Ralph and I found new words to describe our brother Wendell. We had grown up in the years before events like the Special Olympics, or "special ed" classrooms, or movies like "Rainman" and "I Am Sam," so for us, Wendy was always simply "retarded," "our crippled brother." He was "not normal," not like other kids. When the reclassification of retarded people began in the late 60's and early 70's, we were pressured to use politically correct words like "special needs," "handicapped," and "developmentally disabled" to describe our brother.

In our late teen years, military duty and college took Ralph and me far away from California and we lost regular contact with Wendy during his early twenties. After Ralph finished his stint in the Air Force, and had returned to Sacramento, CA, I moved far away to the east coast. For about 25 years I would see Wendy only about once or twice a year for holidays and special occasions. Frankly, while submitting to the demands of young adulthood (marriage, career, parenting), he was seldom in my thoughts (out of sight, out of mind).

When we reached our mid-life years in the mid-1980s, however, all three of us Jacobson boys finally reunited in Northern California, the home of our youth. Ralph and I began talking on the phone with Wendy more frequently and visiting him more often at his designated homes in the Napa Valley. After a long hiatus in our relationship we found a "second life" with our brother, who had melded into an adult man.

Twenty-five years have passed by since this reunion, and now that Wendy has worked his way to the unthinkable age of 70 in defiance of all predictions of a shortened life-span, Ralph and I have near-lifetimes to look back on our years with him as our brother. It has become clearer to us that the "retarded kid" we grew up with is truly a "special" human being.

Even while he was off the radar screen of my own mind during our years of separation, I was occasionally reminded of Wendy's unique place in my personal history. One such time came during a sudden and brief encounter with a neighbor boy in New England in 1978. John had come home from a day at school and, as usual, was waiting for me to return from work to play kickball, or whiffle ball, or hide-and-seek with him and my three daughters, which was a regular afternoon ritual. On this particular day, the girls had gone from school directly to play with friends, so when I came home, I found John alone at the front door of our home, waiting impatiently for the action to begin.

After explaining the situation I attempted to deflect his disappointment by asking, "So, what happened at school today, John?"

"Not much, but something really funny happened at lunch-time."

"Like what?" I asked.

He explained, "Well, they brought in some retarded kids at lunch-time and they sat down right next to my table."

"Wow, what was that like?"

"It was really weird. They were walkin' all funny like this" (John began to imitate the spastic, jerky walk of kids who probably had down syndrome or cerebral palsy) . . .and they talked like this–'na, wha,na, wha, ngh-uh'. It was really funny but a little scary."

His descriptions reminded me of how often, as a child, I had witnessed the curious stares, quizzical looks and attempted mimicking by other children or even adult strangers, as Wendy would walk past them. I thought of the many times I had explained to my friends at school that my brother was just retarded and that he wouldn't hurt them. I don't remember becoming disgusted, or angry or embarrassed by these negative responses to Wendy because Ralph and I had been coached by our parents on how to process reactions to him. They would tell us, "Wendy is not like other kids and these people are not being mean. They just don't understand him. When they get to know Wendy, they'll like him."

With all of this history swirling in the backlog of my mind, I smiled at John and said, "Hey, come with me. I want to show you something." He followed me into the living room of our home and I led him over to the display case where we had placed some of our family pictures. I handed a framed picture to him, and watched as he examined the stooped stance and off-centered smile of Wendy, sitting next to my parents, in front of Ralph and me.

"That's my family–my mom and dad, my brother Ralph and there in front is my brother Wendy. Wendy walks and talks just like the kids who sat down near you at lunch today. He was born with a disease called cerebral palsy, but he's our brother and we love him very much."

John blanched with embarrassment. "Oh, Mr. Jacobson, I'm sorry. I didn't know you had a brother like that."

Attempting to salve his guilty mind, I said, "I know you didn't, John, and I don't want you to feel bad about what you said, but I wanted to tell you about Wendy so the next time you see people like him you will not be afraid. Maybe you will see them as "real people," special people who may even be part of a family like my family."

The impulse for writing Wendy's story has come, in part, from encounters with kids like my neighbor-boy, John, who have been frightened or disgusted in the presence of unusual people like my brother, or who have simply "missed out" on the joy of knowing someone like Wendy.

Numerous friends and family members who <u>have</u> actually met Wendy and have recounted the many moments they have been touched by his spirit, warmed by his love, or delighted by his humor have urged me to write his story. "You ought to tell the world about Wendy," they've said. "He is such a special guy." I am finally submitting to their call, and I write with the hope that many more will be able to enjoy him. . .and other people who are like him.

Perhaps the strongest reason for telling his story, however, is the awareness that Wendy has given more to me and my family than we have given to him. So many of the good qualities I notice in our family, in myself and in my "normal" brother Ralph, have been shaped, to an extent, by growing up with our special brother. This account is a "Thanks" to him for all of the ways he has brightened and enriched our lives.

DAMAGED GOODS

Mom's pregnancy during the fall and winter of 1939 was uneventful. As the season turned to spring, Mom, followed suit and began to "bust out all over" with the promise of a baby. The Community Hospital in Lindsborg, Kansas looked more like a large house than a hospital (some 50 years later it would become a private residence), employing a modest staff of nurses and single small town family doctor. Without any help from sophisticated medical equipment Mom and Dad were promised that the baby would arrive sometime in late June, just in time for the hot, muggy summer season.

Early on June 24,1940, slight contractions signaled that the time had come. "Labor day" was here. When Mom entered the hospital, it was assumed that she would deliver by early afternoon, but it didn't happen that way. The contractions intensified and then relaxed, awakened then slept. Into the late afternoon and evening, an anxious father-to-be, along with his parents and a handful of friends sat out on the porch in front of the hospital and waited. Early evening came and left, then night time came and vanished into the light of sunrise. It was "the next morning" and Mom had been in labor for over 24 hours.

Puzzled, and perhaps concerned over the fact that she wasn't dilating enough for delivery, the doctor decided to wait a bit longer (caesarean sections were not common and a bit risky in this hospital). Another 12 hours passed and then, just after 39 hours of labor, 9-pound 8 ounce Wendell

Kent Jacobson fought his way out of the fatigued womb and struggled to take his first breath. On that day, a baby and a "mommy" and a "daddy" were born.

The sound of their crying baby was enough to drown out all of the screaming worries surrounding this dreadful labor. Besides, it was a boy, alive and seemingly healthy. The Jacobson name would continue. There was excitement in the news-starved town of Lindsborg.

In spite of the marathon delivery and the fact that Wendell's umbilical cord had been wound around his neck, no one seem to be concerned about his physical well-being. He cried like any other newborn baby. He cuddled then fell asleep. When he didn't take to nursing right away the explanation was given that "he just isn't ready. . .these things can take time." Euphoria and relief overcame early concerns, and the new family soon made its way back to their nest on Chestnut Street to begin this new chapter in their lives.

Despite all the family stories that had been told and the "how-to's" about parenting that had been shared with them in the preceding months, Mom and Dad, like every new parent, had to learn how to care for the baby on their own. The fact that Wendell was helpless and totally dependent on them seemed to be normal. Excessive sleeping, fussy eating, daytime crying spells were taken to be "just the way it is" with babies.

The summer months turned to fall, and then winter came. All along, family and friends ooo'd and aaah'ed in the presence of the chubby little newborn. During the latter months of his first year, however, people began to notice that certain developmental milestones were being skipped–his eyes would not follow movement, his head would not stay up on its own, he would not venture to crawl or even attempt "baby talk." The quip that he was just a "late bloomer" began to lose its charm as this first year passed and patience gave way to worry.

Finally, the family doctor weighed in on the matter and recommended that Dad and Mom schedule an appointment in Wichita, KS for an assessment by child development experts, so in mid-summer of 1941 they took the first of what would become many trips to Wichita to meet with the experts. Tests were administered and a follow-up consultation was scheduled. As as Tuggle and Neva waited for the results, hope and worry must have dueled for center stage in their minds.

"He might just be developing slowly," Dad would say. "Maybe we're a bit too anxious."

"What if he doesn't survive?" Mom wondered.

Dad would try to reassure her "He's a Jacobson. He will be okay."

Their hopes came crashing down, however, as they sat in the office of the Director of Child Development to hear the results of Wendy's tests. "We think Wendell is afflicted with a condition called Cerebral Palsy."

"Cerebral what???"

"Cerebral Palsy."

"What is that?"

The doctor explained, "In simple terms, it means that your son was damaged during his unusual and lengthy childbirth. His brain did not get enough oxygen. This may have happened when the umbilical cord got pinched, but because of this deprivation some of the cells in his brain died. We don't know the extent of the damage, or what part of his brain has been affected, but **he will not be a normal child**."

Mom sobbed at the report. Dad teared up and gathered himself to ask the critical question.

"Can anything be done to fix this?"

"Actually, once brain cells have been destroyed nothing can be done to restore them. As time goes on we will know more about what has happened to his brain by watching what Wendy does. Some CPs have normal mental capabilities but their motor skills are affected so they aren't able to walk, or use their hands, or feed themselves. We refer to children like this as "spastic." Other CPs have normal muscular function but the part of the brain that thinks and learns has been damaged. We refer to children like this as "retarded," which means that they will always be like children mentally. Some CPs have had both parts of their brain damaged. These children will be both spastic and retarded."

This news was catastrophic. A bombshell had just blown up in their faces.

"Where do we go from here?"

"Well, you're going to have give Wendell some more time to find out the extent of his Cerebral Palsy. If it is severe, you'll discover that raising a child like this is extremely demanding and frustrating. You may want to consider having him institutionalized. He would be placed in a facility equipped to take care of him so you can get on with your lives. You can't realize what it takes to handle a child like this. Many parents decide that the best thing for their child is to have him or her in a place that knows how to care for kids like Wendell. Think about it. Think seriously about what's best for him and for you."

"How can we give up our own son? How could we live with our son being raised by strangers? What if these tests are faulty and he turns out to be normal?" they wondered.

Again, the doctor tried to console them." I know what you must be feeling, but we are most confident that the tests are conclusive. Wendell will never be normal. You will have to decide at some point if you want to take a chance with him growing up in your home. Maybe you should take a few more months and see if our analysis bears out with your experience, and then come back for further tests."

The drive home, no doubt was filled with emotionally charged discussions about this devastating news. Should family and friends be told, or should we wait until we know more about the damage to Wendell? What if he never talks, or walks, or laughs, or learns? How will people respond? Where do we go to learn how to handle a CP baby and what kind of expenses will he require?

Whirling around these practical issues was the deeper and more private storm of shattered dreams. They had wanted a boy who would make them proud, who would bring them the delights of childhood, a boy who could play with other children, play baseball, go fishing, a child who would grow up to be a handsome, strong, successful man, perhaps even a doctor or professor or a minister. How could this be happening?

Mom and Dad eventually began to face the reality of what the doctors had told them. They had been crushed but were not defeated, and they were not alone. Both of them had been reared in Christian homes where a deep faith in the goodness and love of a sovereign God had been firmly planted. They had learned the stories of Joseph (a Jacob's son) who, after being sold into slavery by his jealous brothers was able to tell them, "You intended evil, but God intended good." They remembered the story of Job, who declared, "Though worms destroy my body, I will see God." They knew the story of an imprisoned Paul, who wrote, "What can separate us from the love of God?" and then answered his own question by declaring that nothing could interfere with God's love.

Beyond this spiritual backdrop they had witnessed how life in the farmlands of Kansas was filled with the inevitable tragedies of nature–the death of animals and pets, droughts, tornadoes, winter storms, fires, illness, and accidents. Mom had even witnessed the drowning death of her sister Merle. They had seen how these tragic events had failed to produce resentment, bitterness and victim complexes. They accepted the biblical maxim that "the rain falls on the just and the unjust."

When they returned to Wichita for a follow-up assessment of his Cerebral Palsy, the doctors confirmed their diagnosis. Wendy was "retarded." He would likely remain as a child, perhaps an infant, for his entire life. It could not be determined for sure, but they told Mom and Dad that he may not ever speak or interact with others, he could be a type of "vegetable." In addition to this, CP had damaged his nervous system. Partial paralysis on his right side meant that he might never be able to feed himself or walk.

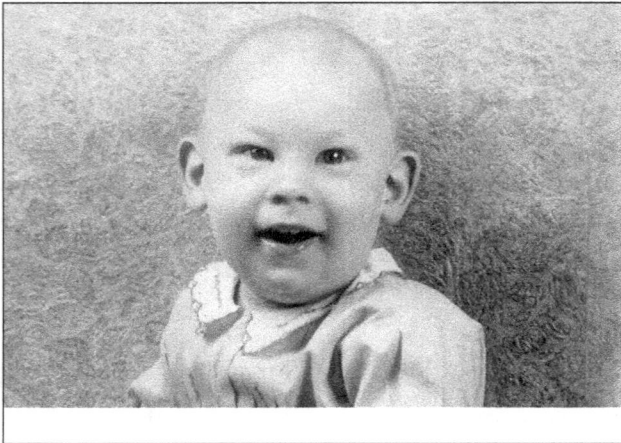

Wendy on first birthday, 1941

The news did not have the same devastating impact on them this time, however, because during the months of waiting, a strong emotional bond between them and Wendy had formed. He was their boy. Their acceptance of his condition had come in small portions measured out over days and weeks, doubtlessly met with many restless nights and days, but somehow they had come to embrace their first-born with the same kind of love and pride enjoyed by parents of normal children. They dressed him up for outings in cute little baby clothes for church and other social gatherings. They held him constantly, and proudly.

Somehow they avoided the impulse to see their baby as "damaged goods," and embraced the challenge to raise this Cerebral Palsy child as a special gift from God. Even so, they were not ready for what would come next.

BAD TO THE BONE

While his parents monitored Wendell's sluggish development, another issue began to worry them. They noticed that his left leg was not growing at the same pace as his right leg. There was a redness and swelling on his left knee. Unusual periods of crying made them suspect that he was in pain beyond a normal call for food or diaper changes. By the time he reached his second birthday, his left leg was about 2 inches shorter than his right leg, so they took another trip to the medical center in Wichita.

Their appointment brought more tragic news. Doctors explained that they would need to take a sample of bone tissue from Wendy's swollen knee to determine why his leg had stopped growing. Wendy screamed as the doctors scraped the bone tissue from his leg, and continued to scream on the long drive back to Lindsborg. The test results would be back in one or two weeks.

Seven days later, doctors revealed their findings, "Your son has a bone infection called osteomyelitis in his left leg. This infection is in the knob of the femur, better known as the "thigh bone," and is affecting the part that grows and lengthens the shaft of the bone, which explains why Wendell's leg is not growing."

"What can be done about it?"

"We're not sure we can stop the infection. However, a recent procedure has been developed where we take bone chips from the tibia (shin bone), grind them up, mix them with penicillin and place the mixture in his knee to stop the infection from spreading. The procedure is painful, but your child is young and we are hopeful that he will do well. If it appears that there are no complications from surgery we'll release him and you can bring him home, but the real proof of success will come several months later when we see that his left leg is beginning to grow again."

Two weeks later, Mom and Dad made the two-hour drive back to Wichita for what would become a seemingly endless series of weekend trips. They waited and prayed as the doctors began the arduous task of chiseling out bone chips from Wendy's right leg. The bone chips were then mixed with a heavy dose of penicillin. They then cut into the knob of his femur, ground out a section of the infected area and packed it with the bone chip mixture. This sequence of surgeries went on for 4 hours.

When the anesthesia wore off, Wendy woke up crying uncontrollably, resisting all efforts to comfort him. Sensing his anguish both parents must have quietly wondered, "My God, why does he have to suffer like this? Wasn't cerebral palsy enough?" Pain medication seemed to do little to tranquilize him as tears continued to flow down his cheeks. He screamed off and on for many hours.

Three days after surgery, Mom and Dad returned to their silent empty home. Daily calls to the hospital let them know that their son was doing well. Daily prayers pleaded for his healing. They would drive to Wichita every weekend for the next three months, and with each visit they could see that Wendell was getting better. Every visit was greeted by his crooked spastic smile and eager reach to be held, and each time they left, he would again cry. . .and so would they.

Finally the day came for his release from the hospital. His wounded leg was enclosed in an ominous cast that stretched from ankle to hip. In those days before car seats and seat belt requirements, Mom was able to sit in the back seat holding and comforting Wendy, which made the trip somewhat more bearable. Though his return to Lindsborg was greeted by a chorus of loving friends and family, the daunting task of caring for a doubly-damaged baby loomed ahead.

After a couple months, when it was time to have his cast removed and his leg examined, more bad news came. The infection was still "alive." There would need to be another surgery, another cycle of pain, another delay, another season of uncertainty. As Wendy was readmitted and a second surgery scheduled, Mom and Dad left again for Lindsborg. This time, the trip home was even more silent and sober than before. Anguish gave way to seething, but as the trip neared its end, they somehow managed to find their center.

"We can't give up."

"He's going to be all right."

"The doctors know what they're doing."

"We must place Wendy in God's loving hands."

A series of crises like this can either drive people apart or drive them together. In the case of Mom and Dad, it evidently did the latter, because around Christmas time of that year, Mom announced that she was again "with child." Consumed by continuing worries about Wendy, the prospect of a second baby must have triggered a new wave of mixed emotions. Will this be another cerebral palsy child? How can we manage a second baby when Wendy demands so much attention? Along side these concerns grew the fresh hope of a healthy child, but preparations for another baby began to work a type of emotional magic on both of them.

Wendell's second surgery proved to be successful and he returned home, again in a full-leg cast. Doctors warned that more work may be needed, but that didn't matter, because the Jacobsons were going on with life and would rise to meet the challenge.

Ralph's arrival in September of 1943 went smoothly. Labor was brief and the baby was healthy. How Mom and Dad managed to balance the demands of a newborn with those of Wendy is not known, but they did. While Dad worked at building up his gas station business, they kept an active schedule with friends and fellow parishioners in the First Covenant Church. They began to speak openly of Wendy's condition and, in doing so, engendered support and admiration from their friends and family. "We have a retarded, crippled son, but he's our son. . .and now we have Ralph. . .two good boys."

One Sunday afternoon in the spring of 1944, Wendy finally rode to Wichita to have his cast removed and happily returned home where Mom had just completed her spring deep cleaning. The freshly waxed kitchen floor seemed like the ideal place for her 8 month old toddler and crippled son to play, but on the very second day of his return as Wendy attempted a couple of steps, he slipped on the shiny, slick linoleum floor and his left leg snapped. Incredibly he would wear yet another cast, enter another season of pain and healing, and wait to walk once more.

Mom's emotional pain during that spring must have been excruciating. Dad had entered the WWII effort and was stationed at Smokey Field Air Force Base in Salina, Kansas, so she not only faced the task of caring for her injured son and her active 8-month old baby alone, but she also learned that she was expecting another baby. Years later she would tell of how she cried for nine months as she carried me. By the time I came "out of the oven" in mid-November of 1944, Wendy was healed, Ralph was walking and the family was finally complete. It was "a wrap."

In spite of his double handicap and broken leg ordeal, Wendy displayed a certain innate spirit of joy and affection, void of bitterness or anger, seemingly unaffected by his early misfortune. He began to show some of the qualities that would endear him to many people during the course of his lifetime. Pleasure in his presence supplanted pity. His early years revealed that he was going to be unique–unlike other children, more stable than many teenagers, more contented than most adults. With two "call strikes" he had begun a journey that would eventually span seven decades and display to many the resilience of the human spirit.

AUTO-MANIA

Imagine not being able to roll, or crawl, or walk until your were 6 or 7 years of age. Picture the confinement of only being able to sit motionless as you watched other kids walking, running, driving, biking, skating, or sledding. This was Wendy's early life. His handicap dictated that he would lie still for the first six years of his life, and even as he finally began to walk, his steps jerky and unsure, movement was slow and precarious. In these first years he must have sensed that because he would not, could not move like other people, and so would need more than shoes. . .he would need wheels.

It was a spring evening, 1947. Our house sat on a quiet street in Lindsborg, Kansas, a short block away from the Petersen's home. Mom and Dad decided to take respite from family chores to enjoy an evening of Pinochle with their friends, while a local baby-sitter watched their 3 small children. The evening went well for the two couples—dinner, games, conversation, a "break" from kids.

But about 7:30 p.m. their mini-vacation was interrupted by the sound of a loud crashing sound coming from across the street. All four adults rushed to the front door, and to their horror, saw the Jacobson family car in a ditch beside the road clinging to a tree. As they rushed outside, to their horror they discovered perched in the driver's seat, their stunned, smiling, crippled son, Wendy. After finding that he was not injured, amazement swallowed shock. Wendy couldn't walk too well. . .but he could drive! No one ever figured out how he had managed to make his way from the house to the car, or disengage the brake, or find neutral gear, or steer the runaway car down toward the Petersen's house, but this event was the beginning of what became Wendy's life-long preoccupation with cars.

No one knows for sure where this obsession originated. Perhaps it was came from the fact that he could barely walk, or because his dad owned a service station and possessed his own fascination with cars, or because the family took Sunday afternoon "joy rides" through the countryside each week, but Wendy developed a consuming love for cars, trucks, tractors, or anything that moved.

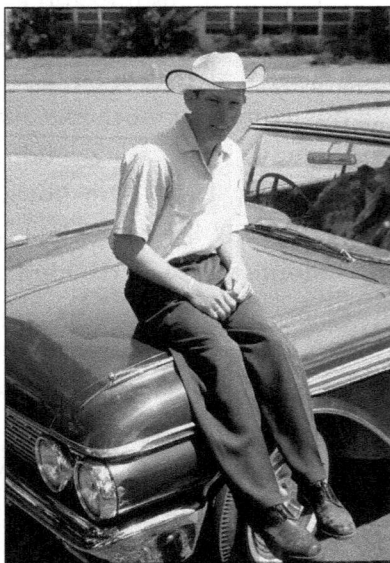

Wendy on our family car, circa 1954.

Later on, during his childhood years, he would wait anxiously until Dad returned home from work each day so he could drive (steer) our family car around the block. This daily routine became the "big event of the day" for him (and perhaps for Dad). An added delight would be the days where Dad could find puddles of water in the street to drive through and spray water onto the sidewalk. Even now, 40 years since Dad left us, Ralph and I have kept this this afternoon driving tradition alive, and although we have added a few more thrills, such as quick acceleration, sudden braking and rapid turning, Wendy's laughter and delight is the same as it was on his very first drive.

Throughout his lifetime, cars have held a dominant place in Wendy's mind in so many ways. For example, he always identifies people not by their names, or their faces, or their positions-in-life, but by the car they drive.

When he tells me, "Wha, wha, I'm see my friend today,."

I'll ask, "O really, which friend?"

"Wha, you know, you know, you know, one who drives black car."

"Oh, you mean Rich?" I'll guess.

"Sure," he'll say.

Cars are part of nearly every phone conversation. If I call him to tell him that I will be coming home in a few days, his questions about my plans are as predictable as the sunrise.

"You, you, you drive truck down?" he'll ask.

"Yeah."

"Wha you park truck in garage?"

"No, I think I'll leave it in the driveway."

He will then give me his suggestions about what to do with my truck, "You, you, you back thing in."

"Okay, I'll back it in," I'll say. It is only after he knows which vehicle I will be driving and where it will be parked, that he can rest easy.

Cars feature prominently in most events that come his way. A couple years ago, when Herb, our 95 year-old step-father, entered the hospital, he was diagnosed with stage-five cancer, and given only a few weeks to live. We met with Wendy to gently break the news to him. We told him that Herb was in the hospital and was very, very sick.

"Wha, wha, wha Herb make it?" he asked.

"Not this time, Wendy. He doesn't have much time left."

After taking a few seconds to process this news, he wept for a couple of minutes, paused and then raised his main concern, "Wha, wha, wha Herb do with his car?" We told him about the possible arrangements for Herb's car and only after resolving this issue did he seem to be comforted.

Each Christmas, Ralph produces a photo calendar for Wendy with each month displaying a different member, or members of the family standing by their car. This calendar reminds him of key events coming during the year, but even more importantly it reminds him of which car everyone in the family is driving, for if he sees the car, he will remember the person. Without cars Wendy would be lost.

THE MIRACLE

When Ralph and I entered our active childhood years, Wendy could only watch as we learned to ride tricycles, scooters, bikes with training wheels and eventually our own bicycles. Caught up with our own delight, we were unmindful of the yearning he must have had to feel the wind on his face, the rush of racing downhill, or the thrill of balance while pedaling.

In 1949, Dad announced that he was taking an offer to work at Barksdale Air Force Base near Shreveport, Louisiana, so our family left Kansas for what would become the first in a series of career-related moves. While settling into a new job, new home, new church and new culture, Dad took on an unimaginably wild project. He set out to teach Wendy how to ride a bicycle. With the echoes of Wichita doctors' gloomy forecasts ringing in his ears ("He may never be able to walk") and his awareness of Wendy's struggle to take even a few consecutive steps, Dad came up with the ridiculous idea that his crippled son would someday ride a bike.

As the project began, Ralph and I smirked with skepticism (as did everybody around us) but eventually we got "on board" with the dream and anxiously waited and watched to see if Wendy could ever ride a bike. Each afternoon after work, Dad would take him out into the street, lift him up onto a used bicycle he had bought, place his feet on the pedals and walk him up and down the street in front of our house. This first phase went on for weeks. Wendy's legs didn't seem to understand the movement of pedals (they barely understood the movements for walking) so Dad would pin one foot to one of the pedals while he pushed the bicycle. Then he would move to the other side to hold the other foot onto the other pedal. Whenever Dad let go, Wendy would fall, get back up onto the bike, only to fall again. He fell hundreds of times over the course of these weeks.

I don't remember the actual day, but we all remember "the event." Dad rounded up the family, took us all out into the front yard and yelled, "Watch this!" He lifted Wendy onto the bicycle, gave a slight push and we watched in disbelief as Wendy began to pedal while holding his balance. He actually rode his bike down the street (about 12 feet). Dad ran to catch him when his streak ended, then looked up at us all and shouted, "My boy can ride a bike!!!"

In subsequent days, as Wendy's proficiency in riding a bike grew stronger and stronger, he was soon riding with Ralph and me, up and down our street and throughout the neighborhood. None of us knew at the time, but this miracle would liberate, and in some ways, eventually define Wendy for many years to come. Barely able to walk, he would ride a bicycle for over 40 years, opening up a whole new world of friends and experiences that most people like him never know. He had grasped the magic of movement and relished the freedom it offered. In every one of our neighborhoods people would not be able to ignore "that crippled kid on a bike."

During our teen years, when we lived in the Town and Country Village area of Sacramento County, all three of us would ride our bikes each day after school, often pedaling up to the "The Village," where we could get a 10-cent A & W root beer that was served in chilled mugs. On one of these trips, Wendy discovered a fire station that was located adjacent to the shopping center. Fascinated by all the flashy red fire engines and trucks there, he soon began making regular visits on his own. After several weeks of his daily visitations, Dad went up to see if Wendy was becoming a pest. The firemen reported that they loved having him around and that if they were busy he would always leave willingly. In fact, he had become their "firehouse mascot."

One hot summer Sacramento day, Wendy returned home from the firehouse dripping wet.

"What happened to you?" we asked.

"Wha, wha, wha, Jack Henry squirt me off. Him, him, him wash off fire truck and my bike," he explained.

After further investigation, we learned that he would often bug the firemen to let him help wash off their fire trucks, and that this engine-washing ritual had developed into a delightful game for the firemen. On hot summer afternoons, after their fire trucks were washed, they would send Wendy across the little side street to a vacant lot and shoot some of their high-pressured water across the street to cool him down. He loved being dowsed and the firemen loved it as much as he did. In fact, some 35 years later when we put on a 50th birthday party for Wendy, two of these firemen drove about 25 miles to join the celebration and to tell some of these wonderful stories of the days during the 50s when Wendy rode his bike up to the firehouse.

Later on during the mid-1960s, some of my college friends were able to learn first-hand about Wendy's attachment to his bicycle. I was in the Biola College quartet, singing in churches and summer youth camps throughout the western half of the United States, and since each of us could appeal for certain concert locations I arranged for the group to sing in my "home church" in Sacramento. I'll never forget the first summer I brought the quartet to my hometown.

As we headed toward Sacramento, I briefed the guys about my unusual brother. None of them had ever been around people like Wendy, but because they knew me they seemed ready to embrace my brother, and as many before them, they soon became enamored with him. During our "Sacramento gig" the quartet logged many hours with Wendy. He became one of our biggest fans, and we became some of his biggest fans.

Years later, Rich Buhler (nicknamed "Cotton), our first tenor, told me that his exposure to Wendy had had a profound impact on his life, because he was able to see what a powerful impact a loving and open family could have on a person with such severe limitations. On that first visit, Cotton picked-up on Wendy's fascination with cars, so he invited him to go for a ride to the store in his VW "bug.". As they rode along, Cotton revealed that he was planning to get married in the fall right after the summer quartet tour. Wendy's main concern about the marriage, of course, was what marriage would mean for the car situation.

"Wha, wha, wha, wha you get married, you have two cars?"

"No I think we're going to keep just one car. What about you? Do you have a girlfriend?"

"Sure."

Cotton responded with a question, "Well, if you were going to get married will you have 2 cars?" Wendy paused to think for minute, then smiled and said,

"Two bikes."

For nearly 45 years Wendy rode his bike. During his 40s and 50s he rode two to three miles each day to some sort of job or day program. Every Sunday he would ride five miles to church and then back to his home again. It was only when he reached his mid-50s that time and gravity conspired to limit his ability to ride. His left foot began to wander off the pedal so he would compensate by forcing his right foot to do most of the work. Falls became more frequent and he reluctantly showed signs of chronic pain in his legs.

The day came when it became apparent that he could no longer ride his bike. A year of frustration ensued as he attempted to maneuver a manual wheel chair. Then with the closing of his group home, we arranged for Wendy to move back to Sacramento. He settled into a skilled nursing home called "The Garden," where Social Services responded well to his transportation needs and after several months we learned that he qualified for a new form of mobility–a battery operated scooter. He once again had "wheels."

For over 20 years now, since retiring his bicycle, Wendy has driven his little red scooter (his "Cadillac") every day of his life. He can be seen on any given day puttering down to Starbucks or driving around his apartment complex and his neighborhood. His rig is equipped with license plates, headlights, a horn, a coffee mug holder, a canvas top, and a partly-filled water bottle to extinguish his cigarettes. Because he has not been willing to sit, his life has been a "moving experience" of exploring the world around him. He would not sit still, he would not be "stuck" in the prison cell of disability, he would not give in to a flawed sentence of "stillness." His ambition to move challenges those of us who reluctantly accept our limitations as an excuse to abandon our dreams of freedom. Wendy's mobility is the kind of miracle about which we all dream.

GIRLS, GIRLS, GIRLS

Puberty crept up on all of us Jacobson boys, just like it does on every boy. Even though Wendy was three years older than Ralph and four years older than me, we did not look to him for help in understanding the emotional and sexual storms that were raging in us during our teen years. Neither Ralph or myself, or our parents considered the fact that hormones were indiscriminate and unstoppable, or that they would "attack" the bodies of mentally disabled people as well as the bodies of normal, healthy boys.

When this "puberty thing" hit, hair began growing in unusual places, nocturnal emissions erupted, and our thoughts suddenly shifted from cars and sports to girls. Dad did take time with Ralph and me to explain a bit about the changes we would experience as we made the transition from boys to men, but I don't know if he ever talked with Wendy. In fact, since Ralph and I could barely grasp what we were being told, how could Wendy be expected to understand? Even with Dad's "short course" in sex education, the metamorphosis we were experiencing was mystifying and sudden. How much more puzzling must it have been for Wendy???

Whatever his level of understanding, he did come through his adolescence owning a genuine fascination with girls and women. Our church consisted of many young couples like our parents, so as our family became more involved in church activities, Wendy became more and more attentive to a number of young women—college-aged girls, young mothers, even our pastor's wife (who was drop-dead gorgeous). He somehow got the phone number of Mary LaRue, and learned how to call her each day. Mary, and others, felt compassion for Wendy and gave him a lot of attention, extending kind gestures of affection to him. This "village effort" seemed to keep him satisfied during his early adolescent years.

But when Ralph and I left home for the military and college, Wendy found himself "home alone" with Mom and Dad... and his hormones. We only heard sketchy details about this time, but we knew that for our parents, life with Wendy had become more and more difficult. It is likely that Wendy was confronting the reality that he was not completely like us and would not be able to experience the teenage thrills that Ralph and I were enjoying–cars and girls. In some ways, his attraction to beautiful women in our church was his attempt to live vicariously through us.

I went off to college and began to date a girl named JoAn, who later became my wife. She was beautiful. After a couple years went by, the time came to "bring her home to meet the family." I drove up early from college to help prepare for her visit. My folks knew the story on Jo, but it was left to me to tell Wendy about this girl I was about to marry and who was coming to stay in our home, so I decided to give Wendy a little pop quiz on morality.

"Wendy, JoAn is going to be sleeping in our house for a couple of nights, but there's just one problem–we only have two bedrooms and there are three of us. She's going to have to sleep with you or me. I'm going to flip a coin. You call 'heads' or 'tails' and if you guess right, you'll get to choose who <u>has</u> to sleep with her tonight."

I flipped the coin and he called "heads." It was "heads."

"Okay, you won the coin toss so you get your choice. Do you sleep with JoAn or do I?" I asked.

Wendy gave me that wry, subtle smile of his and said, "Wha, wha, wha, you turn <u>tomorrow</u> night." I had to let him down easy with the fact that she would have her own room and he would have to sleep with me both nights. Talk about a "hormone freeze."

Earlier, while at the Sonoma State Hospital for the developmentally disabled, he had found his own dating wings and had captured his first girlfriend, Ethel. She was like Wendy. They seemed to enjoy each other's company as well as the social events at the institution–dance parties, game nights, movie nights and outings–and besides, Ethel smoked cigarettes. This love affair went on for several years until Wendell, like all the other residents, was sent to a private "group home" in the Napa Valley area. We never heard what happened to Ethel, but Wendy remembers her as his first legitimate girlfriend, his "first love."

Then, in the late 1980s Wendy returned to Sacramento to live at "The Garden" and shortly thereafter began a love relationship with a girl named Rosie. Their romance would last almost 10 years. Rosie was nearly 15 years younger than Wendy and, like him, had been born with Cerebral Palsy. She was severely spastic, confined to a motorized chair with her wrists strapped to the armrests to keep them from flailing. She could not speak words, but communicated with eye movements and grunts, well enough for the staff and her family to understand what she needed or wanted. Eventually, Wendy seemed to understand her, as well.

He spoke of her pretty brown eyes, her long flowing hair, her soft skin, and everyone in his world could sense that he really did love her. I would occasionally pick up Wendy for a little outing in my car and Rosie always seemed to be with him in his room watching daytime television. I would play around with them for a bit, kicking Wendy in the butt or tossing him down onto his recliner, and would Rosie throw back her head drooling with delight. On one particular occasion, Wendy said to Rosie,

"Wha, wha, wha, I'm goin' with my brother. I see you later, Honey. Wha, you, you, you be alright?"

She grunted, her head bobbed upward and her eyes rolled. I couldn't tell if she was wincing in pain or smiling.

"What did she say?" I asked.

"Her, her, her say 'Have good time.'"

The summer days in Sacramento could be very warm, 110 degrees plus, and the Garden had a poorly run air conditioning system. Wendy finagled one of the staff to put a small plastic child's swimming pool outside on the patio in front of his room. I had seen this pool before but didn't understand its purpose until another day when I dropped in after work on a hot summer day. Wendy was not outside, so I went inside to look for him. As I entered into the main lobby, I saw him slowly shuffling along behind Rosie's chair, pushing her down the hallway toward his room. I followed him quietly. He struggled to turn the corner into his room, opened the patio door and wheeled her chair to the outside. I watched as he moved Rosie up to the edge of the small pool. He then stooped down and slowly removed her socks, gently placing her deformed feet into the cool water.

"Wha, feel good, honey?" Rosie flailed with delight as Wendy sat down in a chair nearby. He smiled proudly and lit up a cigarette.

A couple years later, Rosie's health deteriorated and after a series of infections and medical procedures she was admitted into Sutter General Hospital and placed in their intensive care unit. Her mother and sisters had been faithfully involved in her life, including Wendy in their world as if he were a legal son-in-law. In months prior to her fatal illness they would come by the Garden, load Wendy's wheelchair in the trunk of their car, drive to the hospital and wheel him in to see Rosie. One October morning, Rosie's mother called me to report that the doctors were not holding out much hope for her recovery. She had but a few days to live.

I decided to take Wendy over myself so he could see Rosie one last time. Upon arriving at the hospital, we somehow avoided any visitor restrictions in the ICU ward and I was able to wheel Wendy into Rosie's cubicle. She was in a coma, breathing through a ventilator, fed through clear plastic tube, her arms gently strapped to the bed rails. She looked peaceful. I watched as Wendy scooted up as close as possible to Rosie. He leaned over and took hold of one of her mitten-covered lifeless hands.

"Wha, wha, wha, wha I love you so much honey. You get better, please. Wha I'm love you so much." That was his "good-bye."

As I wheeled him out, he looked up to me and knowingly reported, "Wha, Rosie might not make it."

"I don't think so, Buddy. She's been a good girlfriend to you but her time has come to leave. She's on her way to heaven to wait for you."

At that point, he began to sob and sob and sob. When we got to the parking garage he asked me to stop for minute. "Wha, wha, I'm need a cigawreck." After smoking a couple cigarettes in silence he signaled that he was ready to go home. Rosie died the next morning.

Since Rosie, Wendy has not had a girlfriend. Her picture sits proudly on his bulletin board on his bedroom wall. Though he has made friends with many girls at his apartment, at Starbucks and at his church, I think he may know that Rosie was the "true love of his life." Even in the face of diminished capacities and abbreviated skills, Wendy tasted the joy of human love with her. . .and experienced some of the "wonder" of girls.

"CIGAWRECKS"

We grew up in a culture of cigarette smoking. School teachers smoked during recess, national leaders smoked at press conferences and public sessions, doctors smoked in their examination rooms, all movie stars smoked all the time. . . and our dad smoked. Ashtrays occupied every room of our home and our days began and ended with the smell of coffee and smoke. Some of our early pranks involved hiding Dad's cigarettes or "plugging" a few of them with treated "popper sticks" that would explode upon contact with fire. None of this seemed unnatural or distasteful to us, in fact, we sort of admired Dad for standing up to the stigma against smoking (especially in church). He was like a John Wayne or the Marlboro Man to us.

Even as medical reports on the hazards of smoking worked their way into public discourse and warning labels started to appear on cigarette packages, our father remained resolute in his habit by proclaiming, "Notice, it says that smoking <u>may</u> be harmful to your health." Our brief years in the southern "tobacco country" of Louisiana only served to bolster his nicotine addiction. It was a place where a majority of people approved of tobacco. Even at church, sinners and saints alike would rush to the outside immediately after service so they could "light up a smoke" and discuss the sermon. Our family was put in charge of cleaning up after the Sunday morning services, and, of course, this involved sweeping up the dozens of cigarette butts that had been discarded in front of the church.

When we moved out of tobacco country and landed in a couple of good lively Baptist churches that were unfamiliar with Southern lifestyle, we discovered church cultures that were entirely different from that of the South. One of the tenants of faith of these churches was that committed Christians should be "morally pure." This actually meant that we were to avoid what were known as "The 5 Baptist Sins"— alcohol, dancing, movies, card-playing and, of course, smoking. What a shock for us, and especially for our father!

Dad was great with kids. He coached little league baseball, played basketball, football, tennis with us and with many of the neighborhood kids. He taught Sunday School at our church. All of our friends loved him. But one day, the leaders of the Arcade Baptist Church met and decided that Dad was unsuitable to teach Sunday School because of his "bad habit" of smoking. I suppose they thought that their decision might help Jake to stop smoking, but it didn't. He stopped teaching instead.

None of us boys were tempted to take up smoking during our childhood or youth, although after leaving home, Ralph had a brief smoking stint during his military career and I took up smoking a pipe in graduate school. But soon after he left home in his early 20s, in the tradition of our father, Wendy became a life-long smoker. I remember the first time I saw him with a cigarette in his mouth. We were sitting at a picnic table in Sonoma, CA. Wendy was about 22 years old. I watched him light up. He gave me a glancing sheepish gesture, and then leaned back proudly, as if to say, "Look at me, I've grown up. I'm just like Dad."

And just like Dad, Wendy has resisted the efforts of many people to get him to stop smoking—his care-givers, his friends, his mother, his social workers, and other health-conscious friends. During his years at "The Garden," a skilled nursing home facility where Wendy lived for over 10 years, we attended many "staff review" sessions designed to work with Wendy on any number of domestic and developmental issues. At each session the issue of smoking came up.

"Are you ready to stop smoking, Wendell?" they would ask. Each time his response was consistent. "Wha, wha, wha, I'm think about it."

One day, a few years back, I took Wendy out in my car to run an errand and spend a little time with him. On the way home he ask me to stop and get him a pack of "cigawrecks." As we were pulling into the service station parking lot and I told him that it was going to cost him some money, so he handed me a dollar bill.

"Hey, buddy, nowadays cigarettes cost 3 bucks, not 1 buck," I explained. He gave me one of his knowing smiles, handed me another dollar bill and said, "Wha you get me 2 packs." I thought later, "He's not so dumb after all."

On another occasion, Ralph and I took Wendy out to the cemetery where our dad was buried. We walked out onto the grass near his grave and all sat down together to talk about our father.

"What do your remember about Dad, Wendy? Was he a good dad or a bad dad?" I asked.

"What him good dad. Him let me drive car."

After a few moments of reminiscing about our father, Wendy laid down with his ear close to the grass near Dad's grave as if he were listening to something.

"What do you hear. What is Dad saying?"

"Wha him feel okay."

I took the opportunity to test his love for Dad by saying, "Maybe the best thing Dad did for you was to teach you to smoke. I think you should leave a little something to thank him for that. Why don't you leave your pack of cigarettes here on the grave for Dad so he can have a smoke when we leave?"

Wendy contemplated my suggestion for a minute, weighing the loss of a pack of cigarettes with his love for Dad, then composed himself and replied with some hesitation, "Wha, wha, wha, Dad be okay." He then put his cigarettes safely back into his pocket.

Wendy on a normal day, 2010

Currently, Wendy rides his red scooter around the neighborhood every day. On-lookers cannot help but notice this little old man slumping over the handle bars of his scooter, his toothless lower jaw casually jutting forward, his coffee mug carelessly swinging on the basket in front of him, with his signature pose–a "cigawreck" dangling from his mouth. I am not sure about all the studies on smoking, but I do know that my brother smokes a pack-and-a-half of cigarettes a day with utter pleasure, never exercises, could care less about health issues, and even while possessing a potpourri of disabilities is living into his 70's. Maybe there is more to "cigawrecks" than meets the lung.

DOCTOR DREAD

Wendy has always hated doctors and hospitals, and it's no wonder. Look at his start in life. His early years were filled with pain and isolation from his parents, and all of this trauma was at the hands of physicians. As he grew older and, even though everybody seemed to accept that kids got sick, fell down and got hurt, wore bandaids, had to go to the doctor, and sometimes needed medicine, Wendy never ever accepted these things. From earliest times he resisted any idea that he was sick or hurt, because any such event might mean that he would "have to go to doctor." He had been there, and it was <u>not</u> pleasant.

I remember one such incident that took place in our home in Sacramento during our teen years. We had a small garage-bathroom that consisted of a toilet and sink, which was used exclusively for "peeing" and "pooping" and washing our hands when the main bathroom was occupied. One day, during our teen years, a wave of influenza had swept through our school and both Ralph and I had been struck by the flu. Shortly thereafter it "hit" Wendy. When he felt the rumble and confusion of stomach flu, he made his way quickly, one afternoon, to the garage bathroom and proceeded to throw-up. As I opened the door and witnessed the final thrust of vomit coming from Wendy's mouth, I watched quietly as he stood up quickly, with a surprised look on his face.

"Are you, OK, Wendy?" I asked.

"You bet. Wha, me feel great!" I decided not to press the issue. I simply helped wipe off his chin and walked him back into the house.

Such denial about illness has marked Wendy's life. Though early on he doubtlessly experienced the pain of many common childhood illnesses (colds, flu, sore throat, growing pains) and more recently as a 70 year-old man, the pain of arthritis, in-grown toenails, headaches, urinary tract infections etc., he has never freely admitted to or complained about illness or pain.

A few years ago, Wendy was getting out of the para-transit bus that transported him to and from his daytime job. The driver mistakenly forgot to set the emergency brake, so as Wendy stepped down, the van rolled back, knocked Wendy to the ground and rolled over his leg. He was rushed to the Emergency Room, where it was discovered that he had a small fracture, unfortunately on his "good leg." He was admitted into the hospital.

I knew how traumatic this might be for him, so I went immediately to the Medical Center where he was staying. When I arrived, I was ushered into his room just in time to witness an interview being given by the physician assigned to him. The doctor was a young asian man, programmed to conduct "indemnity-proof" in-takes and obviously unacquainted with mental disabilities. In difficult-to-understand English, he asked Wendy the usual questions (name, age, address, etc.) and then weighed in with some heavy technical medical jargon.

"We going to take some X-rays of your leg and put you on some intravenous pain medication. This may involve some serious side effects, such as light headedness, disorientation and possible cardiac failure. We are going to set your leg in a soft cast. You will have to stay off your feet for one to two weeks. The hospital cannot bear any liability for your decision for your treatment. Do you understand what I've told you?"

I felt sorry for the doctor. Beyond his normal quizzical expression, Wendy looked as if he were in a stupor. He kept glancing up at me during the interview to see if I understood. I kept smiling and nodding. Finally he responded confidently to all the questions by saying, "Sure."

Immediately after this interrogation Wendy voiced his main concern, "Wha, wha, wha, me have cigawreck?"

Stunned by the question, the doctor hesitated for a moment, then responded dispassionately, "Well, we don't allow smoking in the hospital."

Wendy thought for a second and then pursued the issue a bit further, "Wha me, me, me go back to, to, to, to place out back??

I clarified for the doctor, "You mean the loading dock, Wendy?"

"Lo, lo, lo, lo, loading dock," he affirmed.

The doctor recused himself, "Well the nurse will have to help you with that. Meanwhile, if you consent to our plan, we'll get you started on your treatment."

"Wha, wha, wha, OK."

Wendy was to be in the hospital for 4 days, so I visited him the next day and found that he had won over the nursing staff completely. They loved him. He had, no doubt, been bugging them about smoking, so when I arrived I immediately asked permission to take him out for a "nicotine fix." They kindly arranged for a "bed-on-wheels" and loaded him up for the "Marlboro trip." I pushed him to the elevator, down to the ground floor and out into the courtyard, which happened to be clouded in fog and very cold weather. I offered Wendy his first cigarette in 24 hours. Even with hands shaking he managed to light up, and before the first cigarette was finished, he gestured for a second, then a third, then a fourth, lighting each new cigarette with the previous dying cigarette (an unbroken chain of relief). As I wheeled him back inside he told me he never wanted to go to another hospital as long as he lived, "N, n, n, n, never. N.O. spells 'no thank you'." I hoped he never would.

This trauma only served to reinforce his hatred of doctors and hospitals. Even now, at age 70, when Wendy has a cold and is coughing and sneezing and his nose is running, I will fish for a confession, "Hey, Buddy, sounds like you got a cold."

After a brief pause, he will offer his standard response, "Wha, not me. Wha me feel great!"

"But do you have a <u>little</u> cold? A teeny, teeny, tiny cold?" I'll ask.

Occasionally, once in a great while, he will break and admit, "Jus,' jus,' jus,' little bit."

I reassure him, "OK, take care of yourself. You're going to be alright. Looks like you won't have to go to the doctor after-all". . .and he smiles.

Somehow he has learned to remember the sources of pain in his life and choses to avoid them. I am still not sure if this manner of coping should be called "avoidance" or "denial". . .or "wisdom." Whatever it is, he remains happy and content at age 70 as he repeatedly declares himself to "feel good." I sometimes think of Wendy when I find myself complaining about my own minor aches and pains, and wish I were more like him.

THE DISABILITY "HAT TRICK"

It was a balmy spring day in Sacramento, May of 1954. The young couples group at our church had planned a Saturday afternoon picnic downtown at McKinley Park. Picnics were in the Jacobson blood. During the "Kansas years" much of our social life had been spent at the city park, playing softball, throwing frisbees and playing tag, and our outdoor fun was always complemented with barbecued hot dogs and hamburgers, potato salad, baked beans and either watermelon or home-made ice cream. We loved picnics.

This particular day was no different. We boys were running around the park with our friends, while our parents stayed in the shade to chat with the other adults and cook. Wendy was sort of a novelty to all of our friends. In our games of tag he was given a little slack when it was his turn to be "it" (he always caught us) and in our softball games he was allowed to swing until he hit the ball, and no matter where the ball went, he made it to first base every time. It was fun for all of us.

Sometime before the food was ready, we heard some of our friends screaming from the far side of the softball diamond, "Something's wrong with Wendy!" From where I was, I could see him lying on the ground. His legs were jerking in a way I hadn't seen before. My dad and a couple other adults ran quickly across the grass and I followed them. When I got to the place where he lay, they were leaning over Wendy and shouting to all of us, "Stay back, stay back!"

I will never forget the horror of peeking through the circle of attentive adults and seeing Wendy's tormented face. His eyes were rolled back with just the blood-shot whites showing. A bubbly drool was coming out of his mouth. His hands and legs were flailing wildly. The seizure lasted about 5 minutes. When it had passed Ralph and I started to cry, partly out of relief and partly out of fear and confusion. Because his youngest sister, Ikey had had epilepsy, Dad knew what was happening to Wendy and knew what to do. "He's going to be okay" he reassured.

I don't remember our parents saying too much about the incident on the way home other than they would have to get Wendy in to see a doctor ASAP, but they must have anguished with some of the same thoughts I had at the time. Why would this happen to Wendy of all people? First he had Cerebral Palsy, then osteomyelitis, and now this? Hasn't he had enough? They probably worried about what the threat of seizures would mean for our daily lives. Could Wendy go to school or church, be out in public, live safely at home? What if he falls and seriously injures himself? How would Ralph and Lyle handle a seizure if they were not there?

That next week Wendy was taken in for more tests and it was confirmed that he had epilepsy. He had just achieved the "disability hat trick." A medication (dilantin) was prescribed and after several weeks of experimenting with his dosage, life-as-normal resumed. I think that Wendy had a couple more seizures during his teen years, but he was told, and evidently grasped that if he would take his pills he would not have to experience any more seizures. He never had another seizure.

I think of how Wendy has managed his epilepsy and compare him to the people who struggle with various physical and emotional disorders (bi-polar disorder, ADD, alcohol addiction, depression, etc.) and who need various kinds of treatment to help control their deficiencies. Many of them resist "taking their medicine." They get stuck in a cycle of "recovery and relapse." They relive the horror of their disease simply because they refuse to accept the fact that they need help.

It is amazing to me that Wendy has kept his epilepsy under control all these years since the crisis of 1954. He rigorously follows his medication regimen. When he spends the night with one of us, he <u>always</u> remembers to take his epilepsy medications at bedtime. If I forget, he will ask me "Wha, wha, wha you have my pills." Even with his stunted mind he has never forgotten his pills. Not once.

I remember working on a high profile job during my work in the sheet metal trade. Our company had installed a sophisticated cooling system designed to maintain optimum temperatures for computer servers that held and transmitted huge amounts of digital communication. Failure to cool these computers would result in millions of dollars worth of loss to the company that managed them. After our installation, it was discovered that the openings for cool airflow were too small. Our equipment could not deliver the required cooling because of the physical restrictions that were in place.

We had a meeting of engineers, contractors and installers to assess the problem. After showing our readings and analysis, the foreman from our company explained that we needed to rebuild the structure to allow for proper airflow and cooling to flow into the targeted space. The general contractor blanched at this assessment and declared, "To change the structure is going to cost me thousands of dollars."

I'll never forget the response of our foreman. He simply said, "Bob, these are the facts. If this is going to work we have to widen the openings. It is what it is." In a way he was saying, "stop thinking about what <u>should</u> be and deal with what is."

I don't think that Wendy resents the fact that he needs to take his medications every night, nor does he show any signs that he is bitter about his epilepsy. "It is what it is." He simply refuses to go back to McKinley Park.

DEATH, WHERE IS THY STING?

It was Christmas Eve day, December 24,1969. Wendy was living in Eldridge, CA at a first-class state-run facility for the developmentally disabled, during the days before Ronald Reagan "privatized" (closed) such facilities. Ralph was living in Sacramento, a few miles from the house we'd all known as "home" during our teen years, and I was living in Denver, Colorado for my final year of graduate school . The tradition in those years was for Dad to pick up Wendy and drive him home so he could be with the family during the Christmas/ New Years holiday. On this particular day, Dad left the house in the morning as usual, while Mom stayed back to get things ready for the celebration. Dad only made it about two blocks from our house when he sensed a crisis, turned the car into a neighbor's driveway and collapsed over the steering wheel. When the medics arrived, Dad was gone. He had had a major myocardial infarction. He was DOA.

I was out in the street in front of our Denver home, hosing off our VW "bug" (painted during a car water-coloring prank by our youth group the night before) when I saw our pastor drive up. He got out of his car slowly, walked up to me and uncharacteristically put his arms around me.

"I'm afraid I've got some bad news for you."

"What is it?"

"I just got a call from your brother, Ralph. Your dad has had a major heart attack. He died this morning."

I was stunned. How could this be? My Dad was so full of life. He had always been there. He was my "rock." He was such a part of me and of us. He defined our family. I was too stunned to weep in that moment. In shock, I thanked Pastor Hanstead and went inside to tell my wife, Jo, and we both wept in anguish and disbelief. I called Mom and talked and cried with her, then called Ralph. We decided that Jo and I would come as soon as possible, so we arranged to fly out to Sacramento the day after Christmas.

When it was determined that Ralph would go down to pick up Wendy on Christmas Day, he asked two other friends to drive down with him because he could not bear to tell Wendy about Dad by himself. After picking up Wendy, the transporters made the hour-and-a-half trip to Sacramento listening to Gospel music and talking about other things. Ralph dropped off his friends, then took Wendy to his own house to tell him what had happened.

"I've got some very bad news. Dad had a heart attack this morning on his way to pick you up and he died. He's gone." Wendy broke into an uncontrollable sobbing. Ralph did as well. None of us had encountered death before this time, so we were not only processing the loss of our dad, but also trying to wrap our minds around the finality and irreversible nature of death.

I'm sure that Ralph searched in his own mind for ways to console Wendy because he knew how important Dad was to him. Finally he said, "You know that Mom really needs you to be strong right now. She's just as sad as we are, and she will need you to help her through this."

After some moments of thought, Wendy responded, "Wha, wha, wha, okay," and then began to ask the obvious questions.

"Where, where, where Dad is?"

"Wha, his car wrecked?

"Where you park car?"

"Where Mom is. Wha, wha, I see her soon."

"Wha, her ask 'bout me?"

Looking back on that time, I've often thought of how self-absorbed we all were in thinking about this tragedy in terms of the loss it meant for us, but when Wendy finally made it home to see Mom, he zoned in on her in an incredible way, as if he were in a trance. I remember watching him stare at her and asking her over and over, "Wha, you be okay? Wha, I'm love you so much." It was as if he was saying, "Dad's gone, but you're still here." She recounted later that her deepest peace and deepest comfort at the time of Jake's death came from Wendy. "No one consoled me like Wendy."

I doubt if he understood or understands death any more than any of us do, but maybe one of his advantages is that he more easily moves beyond the things he doesn't understand to work with the few realities he does understand. Perhaps he lives more in the present and looks to the future clearly enough to escape the seducing self-pity of past losses.

Forty-one years later, Mom died at the age of 92 (she had always said that her main request was to out-live Wendy). On the day before she died, we took him over to see her, even though she was barely conscious and couldn't speak by then. We ushered Wendy into her room. He moved close to her bedside and held her hand for several quiet moments, and then began repeating over and over, "Wha, wha, wha I love you, Honey. Wha, you good Mom." After seeing Wendy, her comforter, she was ready to go and passed away the next evening.

The morning after her death, my wife Diann and I went to tell him that she had died, and again he broke into instant sobbing. His tears lasted for a couple of minutes, and then he reached out to hug Diann, crying out through his grief, "Diann, you, you, you please be my second mother." She was sweet enough to tell him that she would serve in that role. Mom was gone, but he had a new mom. Since then, when he calls he always asks me, "Wha, wha, wha my beautiful mommy doin?'" He occasionally remembers and weeps over our mother, but more often he lives with what is–his living "second mother." "Death, where is thy sting?"

Another encounter with death happened several years ago when our Uncle Kenny from Kansas passed away. He was in his late eighties and had a history of heart-related illness, so his death was not a shock. Wendy hadn't seen Kenny for quite a few years, though he certainly remembered Kenny, his cars and trucks and his humorous antics. When I got word of his death I went over to The Garden to spend some time with Wendy and tell him about his uncle.

"We got some sad news, today. Uncle Kenny passed away."

Once again, Wendy burst into tears. I tried to console him by explaining that Kenny had been sick for a long time, and that now he would get to go the heaven to see Dad and Aunt Ellnette again. After a while, he settled down and began asking about Kenny's car, his house and his dog. When I sensed that the emotional storm had passed, I headed to my car to leave and, as was his custom, Wendy followed me on his scooter to say "Goodbye." When I said "See you later, Buddy," he burst into tears again.

"Wha I'm feel so sorry for Uncle Kenny."

Having exhausted all my efforts to console him, I said, "If I give you a couple bucks, would that help you stop crying?"

"Sure," he replied. I handed him two dollars, he smiled, and I drove off with the satisfaction of purchasing some very cheap grief therapy.

I have come to realize that Wendy's approach to death is wonderful. He grasps some of the finality of death and grieves over his loss, but death does not consume or defeat him. He is more interested in living. Where is your sting, Death?

FRIENDS HIGH AND LOW

Wherever Wendy has lived he's always managed to collect a group of friends around himself. During his early months at the Sonoma facility he would stand each day on the corner waiting for a bus to take him to his day program. A young man, named Alan Beals, drove past that bus stop every morning and began to notice Wendy. One day he stopped to talk and became fascinated with this young, happy-go-lucky disabled kid. As he went inside to introduce himself to some of the staff and inquire about Wendy, he was given permission to take him out for coffee. As the weeks and months went by, Alan regularly took Wendy home with him to hang out with himself, his wife, Darlene, and their two daughters. The Beals became Wendy's "second family," and his bond with Alan took on the qualities of genuine adult friendship, so much so that Alan wrote an article for the local newspaper entitled, "Wendell, My Best Friend." His article described the delight and satisfaction he received by being in Wendy's company, the force of mutual respect in their friendship and the significance of having a devoted friend like my brother.

Serendipitous friendships have sprung up at every stage of his life. The Garden, where Wendell spent over 10 years, during his fifties and early sixties, was located about a block away from "The Pavilions," an upscale shopping center accommodating high end businesses like A Sharper Image, Williams of Sonoma, Ruth Cris Steak House, and of course, a Starbucks. Each day Wendy would drive his scooter down to

Starbucks for a cup of afternoon coffee, and would sit outside in designated smoking areas to drink his coffee, smoke and kibbutz with the locals. Every time we would meet Wendy at The Pavillions for coffee we would be amazed at how many people stopped to greet him, shop owners and workers, security guards and regular Starbucks customers. Often he would display little gifts he had received from his friends, especially on occasions like his birthday or Christmas–bottles of champagne, cupcakes, cigarette lighters, etc

When his scooter had to be in the shop for several days, Wendy was forced to travel in a manual wheel chair, but this wouldn't foil his daily Starbucks routine. I met him at The Garden on one of these "scooter-less" days to push him over to the Pavilions, and as we were having coffee outside, a young, very attractive young woman came out of the clothing store to greet us.

"Let me know when you're ready to go back, Wendy." She then turned to me and said, "I push him back to Garden every day and we have a smoke together. He's my buddy." A fleeting, embarrassing thought slipped into my mind, "I don't think I would even do that for Wendy, at least not every day." What a friend she was!

The Starbucks staff knew Wendy and the kind of coffee he liked–decaf coffee with a shot of vanilla syrup. More often than not, they would see him coming and have his coffee ready by the time he had made his way to the counter. More often than not his coffee was "on the house." A day manager told me once that he had had Wendy fill out a job application. "If he ever needs a job, we want him to work here."

After his years at The Garden he moved into an apartment complex, across the street from my house, one block away from another Starbucks shop. A staff member serving his apartment living told me recently that Wendy knows all the people in the apartment and makes his "rounds" to see them everyday. My neighbors all know Wendy, as do the Starbucks staffers, regular coffee-drinkers, the Midas Muffler workers, and random locals who regularly tour "the hood."

One day, a couple weeks before Christmas, when Diann and I walked down to Starbucks with Wendy for some afternoon coffee, I took his travel mug inside to get a refill. The mug was well worn as evidenced by quite a few dents, chipped coating, and a loose handle. When I handed it to the lady working the counter, she said with a sparkle in her eyes,

"Oh, I know who this belongs to. How do you know him?"

"I'm his brother."

She smiled and said somewhat forcefully, "Well, he really needs a new coffee mug (what kind of brother are you?)."

When I told her that we were planning to give him a new coffee mug for Christmas, she said that she had a favor to ask of me.

"When he gets his new cup, do you think I could have this old one? He's a very special person to me." After a brief moment to process this strange request, I assured her she could have it, and eventually gave it to her.

On another occasion when I took Wendy's travel mug in for a refill, the young man at the counter apologized for not having any decaf coffee brewed at the time and asked me if "regular coffee" would be alright. One cup of caffeinated coffee couldn't hurt I thought, so I said "Fine", took the coffee and turned to walk out the door. The young man stopped me.

"Wait a minute! Is that for Wendy?"

"Yes it is."

"Are you a friend?"

"Well, I'm actually his brother."

He turned to another staffer and said, "Hey Rick, this is Wendy's brother!" They both "perked up." I felt like a celebrity.

Then the young man asked me to bring back the caffeinated coffee and told me that he wanted to fix a "decaf americano" with the espresso machine explaining,

"I don't want to give Wendy regular coffee because, at his age, I'm not sure it would be good for his heart."

I thanked him for watching out for my brother. Sudden memories of the steady gentle stream of Wendy's friends flashed quickly through my mind stirring a mixture of wonder and gratitude at the kindness he has received from so many ordinary people.

Later I thought of what the Beatles' wrote in their haunting song, "Eleanor Rigby." "All the lonely people. Where do they all come from?" The lyrics had resonated with millions of people who were nursing the sting of loneliness in their friendless, self-absorbed world of relationships. If Paul McCartney had only written his song for Wendy, he would have sung, "All the friendly people. Where do they all come from?"

WE ARE FAMILY

When I think of how well and how long Wendy has navigated through life with all of his limitations, it occurs to me that much of the credit for his success goes to our family. Our parents, Ralph and I always included Wendy in most every aspect of daily living. We accepted the way he was, and through the years, we even grew to appreciate and enjoy him (for the most part). Mom used to repeat, during her later years, "I'm proud of all my boys, and I'm especially proud of Wendell." She also said things like, "You know Wendy's not so dumb. In fact, he's probably smarter than the both of you," or "If Wendy had been normal he'd have given you and Ralph a 'run for your money.'"

He remembers every family member's birthday every year, and knows what day of the week on which they will fall. Fifty-one years after his death, we are all reminded each year that Dad's birthday is on February 3rd. Mom's is on March 3rd. The most important birthday, however, is his own, so beginning on June 26th, he starts inviting anyone and everyone to come to his birthday party next June 25th. This big annual event each year is so important to Wendy because it is a time when the family is together.

Our family has not escaped some of the common failures and tragedies of life, however, so Wendy has had to handle losses through a number of broken relationships and divorces among his brothers, nephews and nieces. He has faced the reality of death in both parents, in all of his aunts and uncles and even in some of his cousins, but he has never quite understood why or how people can just leave their family by any means, including death or divorce.

My second wife was very good to Wendy in many ways and showered him with quite a bit of attention. Ten years went by, and then suddenly and unexpectedly, she decided that she wanted to end our marriage and resume her own life as a single person. I arranged for Mom and Herb to meet with me and Wendy so I could break the news to him. As we sat down in a booth at Baker's Square restaurant, I told Wendy that I had some bad news, that my wife was leaving for good and that she wanted a divorce. He instantly broke into tears, crying so hard and loud that many of the people around us turned to see what was happening. He didn't stop crying for some time.

"We're going to be all right, Wendy. You still have Ralph and me and Mom and Herb. You and I will be 'bachelor buddies.'" He finally settled down enough to ask,

"Wha, wha, wha her come see me?"

"I don't know. She probably will. I'm sure she'll want to say goodbye." This hope seemed to allay his sorrow for a time.

She did not go to see Wendy again, nor call him on the telephone. He would call me every day to ask if he could talk with her, and when I told him "No" he would again burst into tears. When the staff at The Garden called to tell me that Wendy was so gloomy that they were concerned about his well-being, I decided to pull out a diversion tactic.

"OK, buddy. We're not going to talk about her anymore. Let's stop even saying her name. Can you do that?"

"Wha, try, try, try to."

This new plan seemed to work well as we started talking about other things like what was going to happen to our car, was I going to keep the house, would he still have a birthday party at the house, etc. Wendy did fairly well in keeping our agreement, but a few days later he called and told me, "Wha, I have dream about someone last night."

I knew to whom he was referring. I wanted to find out if he could refrain from saying the name so I said, "Oh really, who was it?" There was a slight pause.

"Wha, wha, wha me not say. Me keep my mouth shut."

This became his way of disguising his thoughts and sadness about his friend and my wife leaving. I knew he was hurting so I stopped by to see him almost every day for a while. One day we went out to get a pepperoni pizza and bring it back to his patio for dinner. The pizza place had included a few green peppers in with the pizza. As we began eating, Wendy asked me if "somebody" (he knew not to say the name) would come by to see him, and as he asked me I saw the tears trickle down his cheeks. I decided to use another diversion tactic.

"Well she's not going to want to come over here if you're going to be crying all the time."

The tears stopped instantly, as he claimed, "Wha me not crying."

"Well then what are those tears I see on your cheeks?" I asked.

He thought for a split second, then pointed down to the pizza carton, "Wha, wha, wha hot peppers."

Though we have attempted to shield him from all the troubles in our families (partly out of self-interest in avoiding the task of repeating information and offering explanations) many times he has sensed problems in spite of our diversions. One time I had to go out-of-town to visit my daughter Karie, who was then living in Boulder, Colorado. She had been going through a rough time–a divorce, relocation, job worries, etc. I told Wendy that I was going to visit Karie, but didn't mention anything about her problems. When I returned, and he asked, "How, how, how her doin'?" I told him, with fingers crossed, that she was doing well, and that things were "great" with Karie.

A couple of months later, when she came back to Sacramento and wanted to see her Uncle Wendy, she took him out alone for lunch. She told me later that when they sat down at the table Wendy asked several questions about her car and then, as if he knew something about her crisis, said to her,

"Wha, wha, wha Karie, wha I'm worry about you so much."

She had to excuse herself to keep him from seeing her weep. How could he know? What did he know? Why did he know to worry? This variation of a "sixth sense" has surfaced in Wendy quite a number of times over the years. When our family is having hard times, he is "tuned in" and will not dismiss his concern.

He has a way of "hinting" when he wants to make contact with someone in the family. "Wha, wha, wha, wha Kim doin'?" is other words for saying "Would you call Kim so I can speak with her?" Or "Wha, wha, wha you beautiful wife busy?" means "Would you call Diann so I can talk with her?"

Recently, at Easter-time, Wendy asked Ralph what he was doing for the weekend (a hint about being included in the family plans). Ralph picked up on this back-handed invitation and told him kiddingly, "We're going to the Mohave Desert and are going to eat some cactus."

Wendy blinked, turned his head away and then responded, "Wha, wha, wha, you so lucky." This was his way of saying that even if you are eating cactus on Easter, I'd like to be with you.

Somewhere in that diminished brain of his there is a section called "Family." In spite of a very limited capacity for understanding, deduction or conversation, he draws from this part of his brain that senses a connection with his family. He constantly expresses his attention to and concerns about all the family members–how are his nieces doing, how is Lonnie (his only nephew) doing, how are the babies doing, how are Shawna (my new daughter-through-marriage) and the boys doing, which of the family members will be at his birthday, etc., etc., etc. Family is at the center of his consciousness, and as it turns out. . .he is just as important to us.

SUNDAY-GO-TO-MEETIN'

Church was always a very big part of our home. Grandpa Jacobson was a Swedish Covenant preacher, who pastored for 50-plus years in a number of small-town churches in Kansas and Nebraska, and though Dad became the "black sheep of the family" he never left his spiritual roots, or his commitment to the local church. Mom's family religiously attended the small country church in Lund, Kansas, a few miles from their farm, in "the middle of nowhere," and seventeen miles from the nearest town. So from earliest times, our family went to church every Sunday morning and evening. Whenever we moved to a new city or town, the first item on our agenda was to find a good Bible-teaching church. We grew up attending Sunday School, Vacation Bible School and summer church camps.

None of us knows how much of the Bible Wendy understands. How could he grasp the important tenants of the Christian faith such as the Incarnation, Christ's Atonement for the sins of the world, the Trinity, or Salvation through faith in Jesus? After all, most people of normal intelligence carry a secret file of doubts and questions regarding such doctrines. But Wendy, who cannot even spell his own name. . . how could he ever understand or embrace these complicated beliefs?

Nevertheless, Wendy has always loved church, especially the music—hymns and choruses, the choir, quartets, trios and solos—and has even loved the preaching (the louder the better). During our years in Louisiana, when Mom and Dad discovered that there were no Swedish Covenant churches in the South, we settled into a small upstart fellowship called Morningside Baptist Church. The preacher, Levelle Kennedy was Irish by descent, red-headed, fiery and red-faced when he preached. He practiced the "hell-fire and brimstone" style of preaching so common in the South, and he was very, very loud.

Our family took part in a full church agenda of social gatherings, potlucks, picnics, softball games, etc. I remember one such occasion when the social committee held a Sunday afternoon "Shrimp Cook-off" picnic at a local park, which was situated beside a large lake. Many young families attended. The three of us boys were playing with the other kids on the large sprawling park lawn, when sometime before the food was ready, one of our playmates screamed out, "Wendy fell into the lake!!!" I can still see my dad running down the grass toward the water, jumping over an aluminum boat and pulling up his drowning son by the shirt. In a couple minutes when Wendy spit out some lake water and began breathing again, all of us also breathed a sigh of relief.

Wendy would not have blamed his near-death experience on God or the church, but the incident may have made some impact on his own thoughts about mortality. Just a few months after this "picnic trauma," he told Dad and Mom that he wanted to be baptized (more water?). When it came time for his baptism, Dad had to walk him very slowly into the water and the preacher had to hold him very tightly while lowering him into the cleansing stream. He has never lost his fear of water, but in that period of life, he evidently feared Hell more than he feared water. He left Louisiana a "baptized believer."

A couple of years later, our positive church experiences continued in Utah, where we joined another little Baptist church. The services featured a talented, energetic, 350-pound pianist by the name of Johnny. Man, could he pound that piano! It seemed as if the volume of the piano issued a challenge to people in the pews to sing even louder, and Wendy loved the energy this created. He would attempt to sing the "old familiar hymns" along with everybody else. Surprisingly, even to this day he can sing the words to many of those old hymns–"Love Lifted Me," "The Old Rugged Cross," "Amazing Grace," and his favorite, "How Great Thou Art."

For years now, if we are driving along in the car, Wendy will want to sing a few hymns, and surprisingly, he knows most of the words. When our family is together, one of his standard requests is that Ralph and I sing with him in a quartet (the 3 of us). We will get him "worked up" on one of the old hymns that escalate in pitch and volume toward the high climax of the song, and then, on queue. . .we will stop singing, leaving Wendy alone to offer a humorous, growling, off-pitch, excruciating finale to the song. The quality does not matter. He has sung with his brothers.

Though both Ralph and I have "taken a break" from church at times, Wendy never stopped attending. When he lived in a group home, near Santa Rosa, CA, Ralph visited him there a number of times and, on each Sunday visit, Wendy would insist on going to his church. On Ralph's first trip, he was aghast to discover that Wendy was riding his bike 5 miles each way, every Sunday, to get to and from church. Furthermore, he was riding along the Old Redwood Highway, a narrow, curvy, heavily trafficked road, void of bike lanes or wide shoulders.

Currently, a para-transit bus picks him up every Sunday morning and delivers him to Carmichael Baptist Church. The people there love him. They welcome him each Sunday morning, allow him to drive his scooter into the sanctuary, invite him to social events, send him cards and notes, and assure him that they are praying for him. He is part of their "church family." When he calls me on a Sunday, I'll typically ask him what he learned at church that day.

"Ev, ev, ev, ev, ev'rything. Whole works." he says.

"Wow, that must have been quite a service. What songs did you sing?"

Every week it's the same answer, "Wha, How Great Thou Art," or "Wha, Amazing Grace."

I have no clue about how much he understands about God, but I do know that Wendy's life-in-church has played a role in producing some of the wonderful qualities on display in his life. Somehow, the best forces of faith have pushed through his limitations and have worked their way into the fabric of his personality. Somehow, he has avoided all the pettiness and arrogance and hypocrisy common to local churches and has found the goodness in them.

When Shawna, my daughter-from-marriage first met Wendy and got to know him very briefly, she told me something that startled me at first. She said that she could "see the face of Jesus in Wendy." Because I knew so much more about him than she, I was initially taken aback by her comment. But then as I began to reflect more deeply about my brother, I thought about how non-judgmental and unassuming he is, how he loves people unconditionally, how easily he trusts and does not question the love of God, and in that brief moment of reflection, I understood what she meant.

DOGS AND FORGIVENESS

All three of us Jacobson boys grew up with a manic fear of dogs. Since much of our childhood was spent on bicycles in the era before "leash laws" were enacted, we were often chased, and occasionally bitten, by dogs. Both Ralph and I had paper routes and Wendy was constantly out-and-about on his bicycle for much of the time after school. One can only imagine how his jerky peddling and awkward style of riding made for a tempting chase by local neighborhood dogs. We all learned which streets to avoid and how to swerve or pedal faster in the presence of dogs. In addition to all of this "bicycle trauma," our family never had a pet dog, so we never quite got the "man's-best-friend" hype about canines.

Even in our adulthood years we had some unfortunate encounters with dogs. Several years ago, following a family gathering, Ralph volunteered to take Wendy back to his home at The Garden, which was about a ten-minute drive. On the way, he decided to stop at a local car wash. While the car was being washed, they walked through a little waiting area where a young Asian woman was seated, holding a seemingly calm, tame Rottweiler by the lease. Without warning, the dog leapt up and bit Wendy on the ass. The dog-owner was horrified. She explained that her dog had never bit anyone in his life, that he played gently with little kids and was "the best dog her family had ever had" (obviously there was no one in her family like Wendy). What ensued was an eight-hour stint in the emergency room, a rabies shot, a follow-up conversation with the dog owners. . . and a reinforcement of the fear of dogs for both of my brothers.

A few years later, when I fell in love with Diann and we began learning about each other, she casually mentioned to me that she had a dog, a Boxer named Gracie. Fortunately we were talking on the phone, so she couldn't notice that the hair on the back of my neck was standing on end. "I can't wait to meet her," I said with tongue-in-cheek. When I did meet Gracie for the first time, I found a sweet-natured, fun-loving, harmless dog, and in spite of my "dog history" and misgivings, Gracie and I instantly bonded. Wedding plans could continue. I now refer to Gracie as "my dog-in-law," but only later did I learn that accepting Gracie was a critical factor, a potential "deal-breaker" in my relationship with Diann.

I was a little apprehensive the first day we brought Gracie down to my house to meet Wendy. He was sitting on his scooter in the back patio area as we let Gracie run into the back yard. Wendy stiffened a bit, but perhaps the smell of his cigarettes was stronger than the scent of his fear, Gracie ran up and immediately began licking his face.

"She likes you," I told him. "She wants to be your friend."

As the weeks went by they did become friends. Each time we brought her down to the house in Carmichael, Gracie would race toward Wendy, jump up and lick his prickly beard and sniff his tobacco-ridden scooter. He would always give her a big hug, then tell her to get down. He learned to play "fetch" with her. He worried about her getting out of the back yard and became very diligent about keeping the gates shut when she was in the back yard. When we would be away from Carmichael and would call Wendy in the evening, somewhere along in our conversation, he would ask,

"Wha, wha, wha Gracie doing?"

"She's right here, would you like to talk with her?"

"Sure."

At this point, I would bark into the phone (on behalf of Gracie), and tell him, "She says 'Hello,' . . .and her tail is waggin."

He would reply with his own stuttering bark and say, "Wha, wha, wha mine too!"

Wendy and Gracie, 2011.

One day, a few months ago, we found a small irritating lump on Gracie's bottom. A sampling showed that the lump was malignant. The news was shocking to us because cancer is one of the most common life-threatening dangers for Boxers. I took her down to Sacramento to get an evaluation by a veterinarian oncologist and explained to Wendy that I was going to take Gracie to "see a doctor." Without giving him many details, I explained that she had a lump that needed to be checked-out and that she may need a little surgery. His expression took a sudden worried, even panicked form and he asked,

"Wha, wha wha matter with Gracie?"

I told him that she had a little tumor and that we were getting it checked-out to see if was cancerous. Evidently he knew the term, so he asked, "Wha, wha, wha, wha Gracie make it?"

I reassured him that she would be all right, "Oh yes. It's just a test they have to take. She'll be fine."

"Wha, wha, wha you please call me wha doctor say?"

"I'll call you tonight," I reassured.

"Pretty please with cream and sugar on it. You be sure call me, my big brother." he pleaded.

After Gracie had the tumor removed, Wendy began asking each time we would talk on the phone how she was doing. When we would come down to Carmichael, he would genuinely be excited to see her, invite her to stand up on her hind legs to lick his face as he held and patted her back and head. He would often say to her, "Wha, wha, wha, Gracie you wan' come spend night with me at my 'partment?"

Looking at all the trauma with dogs during his lifetime, Wendy's relationship with Gracie intrigues me. Unlike many people who live with residual fears, who harbor resentments from past traumas or nurse memories of frightening moments, he has seemed to be able to dismiss his fear and suspicion of all dogs in the presence of one loving dog. In some ways, he has been able to forgive and forget all the growling, and the snipping, the frightful chasing by neighborhood dogs throughout his childhood. He has even been able to void his memory of the attack by the "car wash Rottweiler." Maybe his limited mind and his reduced capacity to extrapolate or deduce has allowed him the chance for a "new life" with dogs. Oh, that normal people could "get over" pain and prejudice so easily and discover the freedom of forgiveness.

GOOD LOOKIN' MAN LIKE ME

We've never been quite sure if Wendy is aware that he's disabled. My guess is that he either doesn't realize that he is, or he refuses to accept it, because from earliest days Mom and Dad treated him as if he were somewhat normal, requiring him to "carry his load" of responsibility in our household. He had to make his own bed every morning (and still does to this day), he had to put away his clothes, brush his teeth (while he still had teeth), tie his own shoes, and pitch in on the household chores. When it came time for him to start going to school arrangements were made for him to attend class each day, even though the small elementary schools in the 1950s did not have many resources for special needs kids. When the time came for all of us to get jobs, tasks were defined whereby Wendy "work for money." Not cutting him much slack turned out to be a key factor in helping him to see himself as somewhat normal.

At age 70, these patterns of responsibility continue. Though he is beyond retirement age, and in spite of his deteriorating, crumpled body, he still gets himself up and dressed each morning at about 6 o'clock and goes off to work. "Work" is actually a day program for disabled adults provided by the Easter Seal Foundation, but he calls it his "job" and gets a stipend ("paycheck") that we have arranged for him to collect each Thursday. They often give him five or ten one-dollar bills instead of a five- or ten-dollar bill to make his "take-home pay" look a little bigger.

Whenever he comes over to my house on his scooter and I'm busy doing yard work, or washing the car, he always asks, "Wha you need help?" I usually tell him that the biggest help he could be would to stay out of the way. He smiles, and responds, "Wha, okay." Each Thursday, when I'm gone from the house, he will take my large rolling garbage cans from the back driveway, down the private road alongside the house and out to the front street for pick-up, pulling them slowly behind his scooter, and then on Friday he will carefully pull the empty barrels to the back driveway. For a "moonlighting job," he collects aluminum cans, and when he has about 20 or 30 of them he calls Ralph to come over, pick them up for recycling and reward him with a couple bucks for his efforts. Work has been firmly planted in his psyche.

Though he has spent much of his life around other people like himself he has consistently bonded more tightly with staff personnel and the "normal people" in his world. He is actually a bit "snobbish" when it comes to other handicapped people, is not inclined to patronize with them and is often critical of his fellow classmates or roommates.

"Wha, wha him talk crazy all time," he will complain.

"Wha him always fall down."

His own "crazy talk" and faltering walk seem to go unnoticed by himself. In fact, when he began losing what little stability he had, he would often fall to the ground, catching himself with his strong left hand and declaring triuphantly, "Touchdown!" Whoever he speaks with on the telephone, or meets on the street can expect to get an invitation to come over to see him sometime soon, or to come to his birthday party in June. Oblivious to his condition or his looks, he will say enthusiastically, "Wha, wha, wha you come by sometime and see good lookin' man like me."

There have been times when it seemed as if he knew he was different than other people. During the years when Ralph and I were melding into adulthood with girlfriends, cars, high school proms, and eventually careers, Wendy often hinted of a certain jealousy and longing for the things we were experiencing. He would compensate by making his own noble claims on reaching the same developmental milestones by having his own girlfriend, his own vehicle (a bike) and his own job (Easter Seal day program). In his mind he was just like us.

In the late 80's, friends of mine, Duffy and Kelly, gave birth to a sweet little girl named Lauren, who because of some tragic screw-ups by the doctor and anesthesiologist, suffered the loss of oxygen to her brain during birth. She was born with cerebral palsy. Early assessments revealed that the damage was extensive. "Lauren will probably never walk or talk," the doctors told her parents.

Wendy knew about the eminent arrival of "Duffy's baby" and would ask me often if the baby had come yet. When Lauren was born and all of these complications came to light, I told Wendy about her birth.

"The baby's name is Lauren. She had some problems being born. They say she has cerebral palsy."

Before this conversation, I never knew how much Wendy grasped about cerebral palsy, or for that matter, whether or not he knew that he had it. His response stunned me.

"Wha, wha, wha her be like me?"

"Yeah, she's going to be like you," I told him. He sat there for a moment to ponder all this and then began asking me more questions.

"Wha her walk like me? Her talk like me? Wha, wha, wha you call Duffy. I'm want talk with him."

Wendy and Lauren, circa 1998

In the ensuing weeks, Wendy became obsessed with knowing how Lauren was doing. We had to call Duffy many times so Wendy could ask when he could see "Laurens." I remember the first time Lauren came over and Wendy got to hold her. He tenderly stared down at her sweet face and then looked up with a smile of admiration and satisfaction. She was a good lookin' girl. . . just like him.

A BLINDED EYE

I think that the reason so many have been touched by Wendy's presence is that he seems to be blind to any of the idiosyncrasies and oddities that have caused other people to dismiss them. He doesn't see fat, or color, or wrinkles, or pimples. He doesn't smell odor (not even his own). He is not overly impressed by the "stylish," nor critical of the "sloppy." He seems to become more attentive to shy, awkward people and doesn't flinch or frown in the face of peculiar behavior. This spirit of acceptance has doubtlessly come not only from a lifetime of being around unusual people like himself, but also from growing up in a family that tended to accept a wide variety of people, "the good, the bad and the ugly."

When my oldest daughter, Kim, was dating a young black man, she brought him home to meet our family. We were all a little apprehensive about how our mom would respond because she had been raised in the prejudiced culture of a mid-western town that boasted that a "the sun had never set on a black man in Oberlin, Kansas." Perhaps because Kim realized this, she did not arrange for a family meeting with her boyfriend, but she did arrange to take him over to see Wendy. I talked with him on the evening after their meeting and asked him what he thought of Kim's boyfriend.

"Wha, wha, wha I'm like him. Him drive silver car." He continued to ask how Kim's friend was doing and, of course, his main concern was whether or not he would be coming to the birthday party in June. Nothing about color or status was ever mentioned. In fact, in referring to those who roam in his world, he never uses those negative characteristics commonly used to designate people–"that heavy-set woman," "that short guy," "the girl with the thick glasses," "the bald-headed man." Most often, when he is trying to tell us about someone he's seen or talked with, he will use only one critical feature to describe them. . .the color of the car they drive.

As our mother drifted into her late-eighties, she began to reveal the effects of dementia–forgetting recent events or conversations, confusing facts, or responding to comments with a glassy-eyed, confused stare. All of this was exacerbated by a major hearing loss, which she never admitted to her dying day. Wendy no doubt noticed these changes. Can you imagine a phone conversation between a mentally disabled person and a 92 year-old near-deaf woman with dementia? Nevertheless, they would talk on the telephone each evening and often following these confusing conversations, Wendy would call Ralph or me and ask,

"Wha, wha I talk to Mom. Wha her okay???"

Trying to shield him from the full reality of Mom's condition we would respond with comments like, "Sure. She's fine. But you know she's getting older now." Wendy found it difficult to process the fact that the mother, who had always been such a strong, confident woman was in any way becoming debilitated.

"Wha, her not old. Her spring chicken," he would often say. Wendy saw his mother just as she had alway been.

Herb, Mom's husband of 30 years and our step-father, was also showing signs of declining health during this same period of time. He could barely hear. He used a cane or walker to shuffle from place to place, and often chose to anesthetize himself in front of the television rather than engage in group conversation. Wendy noticed the changes in Herb, but was essentially blind to his failing and faltering. On days after Mom and Herb had gone over to see Wendy, we would ask him how Herb looked and he would give his standard replies.

"Wha, Herb do good. Him jus' perky, perky, perky. Wha him come to my birthday party, in June."

When I saw the movie "Shallow Hal," the story of a young man who had been programmed to see the essence of goodness in people rather than respond to their physical appearance, I thought of Wendy. Somewhere lodged in that stunted mind of his is a lens that focuses on the best part of people (even the best part of himself). The Scripture says that "Man looks on the outward appearance, but God looks on the heart." So does Wendy, with a blinded eye.

STUCK

They say that any good quality in a person has a parallel "dark side." For Wendy, this axiom could not be more accurate. He has consistently demonstrated a remarkable drive to overcome his many limitations–riding a bicycle when he could barely walk, communicating his wants and needs through his stutter and stammer, working everyday at a job in spite of a crippled body laced with aches and pains. The dark side of this wonderful quality of persistence, however, is what we call "stubbornness."

In 1952 to 1953, when we lived in the small town Layton, Utah, we rode our bicycles each day to the elementary school, which was about a mile from our house. One evening, a parent of one of our friends called to report a near-tragedy involving Wendy. It seems that while crossing the railroad tracks near our school, the front tire of his bike got caught in the space between the train rail and the asphalt. As the warning lights flashed, and the danger signal rang out, and the guard arms descended, Wendy continued working to free his bike from the train tracks. Fortunately, a school bus driver properly sized-up the situation–"This stubborn little retarded boy is not going to move in time." This perceptive man left his bus, pulled the bicycle from the tracks and dragged Wendy to safety. We never knew the name of this "Good Samaritan," but he had been drafted onto the team of angels charged with watching over Wendy.

For years, our family has often recoiled from Wendy's relentless, sometimes over-bearing push for us to tend to his needs. He is obsessed with calling Ralph and me on the phone each evening and will not rest until he "gets through" to us. One time when I had been away from my home for a few days I returned to discover that he had called me 22 times. I had made the mistake of putting my phone number onto the "speed dial" feature of his phone, so when I didn't answer he deduced that if he kept pushing the button I might just pick up the phone. No answer? No problem. Dial again. . .and again. . .and again.

When some plan or idea gets "stuck in his head" he will repeat it over and over and over, *ad infinitum*. If I return to my home in Carmichael and Diann is not with me, an afternoon patio conversation with Wendy will inevitably ensue.

"Wha, wha, wha you talk with my sweet mother yet?"

"No, but I will. Do you have any messages for her?"

"Te, te, te, tell her I see her very soon. Whe, whe, when her come down?"

"This coming Friday."

"Te, te, te, tell her I'm waiting for her round corner."

"Okay, I will."

You would think that such an exchange would satisfy his quest for information, but no, later that evening he will call and ask the same questions and give me the same instructions. The next morning, he will drive over before going to work and again, we will have the same conversation once more.

Although we have developed some techniques to handle these obsessions, they don't always work so Ralph or I have to play "hardball" in the face of relentless pressure. "Back off, Wendy. You're buggin' me," we say, or "You ask one more time and I'm going to hang up." He'll usually pause for a second, and then comply with a "Wha, okay" (evidently he can bite his tongue even without teeth) but we know that the wheels of his mind keep spinning, the obsession persists.

There have been a number of times when people tending to Wendy have seen his stubbornness escalate into anger, even rage, and have called us with the report that "Wendy has just thrown a fit." He probably holds back on these kind of outbursts with the family, but in his apartment or at his workplace he's been known to "swear like a drunk sailor," or throw things, or even drive his scooter away in anger. In every instance, these episodes have come from events that conflict with something he wants to do and cannot do, or something he doesn't want to do but must do (pretty normal sets for anger).

Recently, the director of his assisted-living program called to tell me that Wendy was "giving the staff a hard time" about taking his nightly shower. He was refusing to let them help him with the ordeal. Coupled with his bladder-control problems, his smoking and normal body odor, his poor quality bathing habit was bringing in complaints about Wendy's stench. The director asked if I would have a talk with Wendy. Here's how that conversation went:

"Hey buddy, I talked with Ryan today and he told me that you're giving the staff a hard time about taking a shower. Is this true?"

"Wha, wha, wha little bit," he said sheepishly.

"A little bit?" I asked. Then without waiting for a response, I lowered the boom. "He told me that you're yelling and swearing at them. This has got to stop! You need help taking a shower, so they can get to all those places that cause a stink. You know what I'm talking about," I said as I pointed to his rear end.

He gave me a sheepish glance and finally said, "Wha, wha, wha, okay."

Wendy had been bugging me about wanting a flat-screened TV, so in a flash of genius, I told him that if he cooperated with the staff for one week, I'd get him a new TV. I also told him that I would be checking-in with the staff each day to see how he was doing on the shower project.

It worked. The staff people were ecstatic over his compliance and the workplace staff was also delighted by his clean body odor. In fact, Wendy has his new TV and has continued allowing the staff to assist him in the nightly "clean up operations." Almost every day he reassures me that he is still cooperating by proudly reporting, "Wha, wha I"m take 3 showers last night!"

Though his obsessions can be irritating (most are) it seems that the trick to loving Wendy through them is to forget about trying to squelch his stubborn streak, but rather choose to manage it. After all, his tendency to get "stuck" has empowered him to "stick around" for quite some time.

NEVER LOOK BACK

The Bible says, "Where there is no vision, the people perish," another way of saying that when people do not have something to look forward to they will cease living. Many of us have wondered about what keeps Wendy going? Besides having a long list of physical maladies, he never exercises, smokes a pack-and-a-half of cigarettes a day, thrives on fast food and packaged dinners, drinks coffee throughout the day and calls for a beer as often as possible, and he has little concern about personal hygiene. In spite of all this, he is living into his 70's, with no signs of fading. I believe that the explanation for his resilience is the fact that he harbors a constant vision, or hope of something good coming his way in the future.

Several annual "big events" are chiseled in stone on his mental calendar and they tend to dominate his thinking and conversation throughout the year. The first annual event is the spring "sleep-over" at my home. When Diann and I married we decided to keep both of our houses, one in Carmichael and another in Oroville. The week after our wedding, Wendy began bugging us about coming up to Diann's house in "Onville" (as he calls it) to spend the night with us, and like idiots we agreed that he could come during the month of April. This plan has resulted in a standing appointment. As soon as Christmas has passed, he begins calling to "nail down" a date for his April sleep-over.

"Wha, wha, when I come up see you in Onville nex' April." This goes on for 4 months.

Then when his April visit has passed, he begins talking about his birthday party in June, which involves a second sleep-over. He must certainly invite hundreds of people throughout the year, though fortunately, only about 25 to 40 actually come. If I have plans to see any person he knows, I will ask him if he has any messages for him or her, and every single time he will give the same response: "Wha, you, you, you 'vite him come my birthday party." As June 25th draws closer, the volume goes up and the invitations pile up. He cannot wait for his birthday party!

When the party is over, you would think that he might experience something of a let-down. Not at all, for immediately he will start talking about the "State Fair sleep-over." Years ago he loved to go to the California State Fair where he would ride the bumper cars, play some of the midway games to win a teddy bear, and then have a sleep-over at my house. As the years went by, it became more and more difficult for him to maneuver through the swarming crowds, so the annual outing morphed into an August sleep-over (still called "the State Fair trip").

Soon after August has vanished, his mind turns to "Turkey Day," then "Chrissom" and New Years, and then the cycle begins again. Wendy is never without a supply of anticipation. His "hope tank" is never empty.

This pattern of expectation also features in his daily life. When I am in town, he will drive his scooter over to my house about 6:30 a.m. where I am typically reading the newspaper, and the first item of business is always what kind of weather he can expect for the day. I will show him the forecast icons showing predictions for the next four days. Fair weather brings a smile, but since he dislikes the prospect of rain and all the inconveniences it brings, the prospect of rain will throw him off for a minute.

"They say it might rain today," I'll say.

He will stare off for a second, and then counter with, "Wha, wha might <u>not</u>."

One day recently, when we were in our winter "wet season," and I told him that the forecast was for rain the next 5 days, he stared off for a second and then countered with, "Wha, wha, wha, may be wrong." Even during a rainy period he chooses to live with the prospect of sunshine.

After he has resolved the weather issue, he will want to know if I will be at the house when he gets home from work, if I will leave out a beer for him, when Diann will be coming down, when Ralph will come over to take him out for lunch, when he can see so and so, when he can come over for dinner, etc., etc., etc. I have watched Wendy's life sustained and driven by hope–every day, every week, every month and every year.

He is even aware of "the big hope." On the day before he turned 70, I conducted a little back patio interview with him. After asking him to reflect on his 70 years (which yielded very little information) I ask him if he thought if he would make it be 100 years old.

"Wha, wha, wha try, try, try to," he claimed.

Then I gingerly broached the subject of death by saying, "You know, Wendy, everybody grows old and someday has to die. Look at Rosie, Dad, Mom, Uncle Kenny. Someday I'm going to die and so are you. Right?"

He pondered these great realities and then said, "Wha, wha, wha, wha me see Dad someday."

It seems as though Wendy is not that interested in looking back into the past because he needs so much time to look ahead. His mantra is, "Wha, wha, me keep goin'." He often tells me or Diann, "Wha, wha, wha I love you res' my life." He is locked in to the future.

STAFF AFFECTION

For some 50 years now, Wendy has been under the daily care of people who serve in the social service industry–institutional staff, group-home staff, nursing home staff and independent-living staff. These workers are surrounded by a cadre of administrative professionals who provide many other resources for safety, health care, transportation, developmental programs, and other supportive services. The paperwork alone for these endeavors is astonishing.

The many times Ralph or I have taken Wendy to our homes for meals or sleep-overs we get a taste of the amount of "work" it takes to care for him. He needs help getting from place to place, assistance in bathing, dressing, eating and performing normal bathroom functions. Beyond these menial tasks of everyday living, he "stews" about his scooter, which usually needs some sort of repair, cleaning or enhancement, and these concerns have to be addressed. He constantly checks on the status of his cigarette orders, his mouthwash supply, or clothes that need cleaning or mending. He usually has a list of "to do" items for his apartment–rearrange his bulletin board, fix his television set or stereo or telephone, get a tablecloth for his patio table, etc., etc., etc.

We are, and have been heavily involved in Wendy's life both inside and outside of his living facilities, but a majority of people like him have little family support. The weight of caring for them is tremendous and it falls on the people who serve them, many of whom work for minimum wage, with minimum training, and yet, they do it all. This work takes its toll, and though the turnover rate is high and burnout is common, many staffers faithfully stick with the task for months and years. I have many good memories of the people who have stayed.

During his first venture from home, Wendy landed in the Eldridge State Hospital, a state-run institution for the mentally and physically disabled. The facility consisted of an expansive constellation of red-brick buildings, enclosed by black wrought iron fences and accented by beautiful old-growth trees and sprawling green grass lawns. From a distance the buildings looked a bit like an ivy-league college, but as one came closer, it looked more like a campus that had been closed down for code violations–chipped paint, eroded grout, moss-stained brick. Inside, however, a clean and fairly inviting (apart from the institutional smell) residential facility could be found. Several hundred "patients" slept in large dormitories that resembled military quarters. They were well-fed in large cafeterias, their clothes were laundered, and a large variety of programs were provided for them–arts and crafts, sports, work projects, outings, and in-house social events.

On my first visit there, I arrived on a day when the place was abuzz with excitement. Everyone was getting ready for an afternoon dance. I found Wendy sprucing up for the occasion in his dormitory bathroom. along side several other residents. He seemed happy and excited and introduced me to one of his roommates, Mike, who was symmetrically paralyzed, as evidenced by his tilted stance, his limp right hand, and the slightly collapsed right side of his face. Most noticeable was that the left side of Mike's hair had been combed nicely while the right side remained terribly unkempt as if it had just risen off the pillow after a restless night of sleep.

"I, I, I, ready. L, L, L, Let's go to the dance, Wendell," he announced as he shuffled away, unbothered by his partial grooming. Wendy looked comparatively handsome, I thought.

I mingled with the staff while watching an amazing dance of irregular people twisting and turning and stumbling to the familiar pop music of the 60s. One man, in his mid-forties struck up a conversation, and I learned that he had been on staff there for just a couple of years. He told me that he had come to work at Eldridge after teaching for several years in the psychology department at the University of California, because he had gotten "fed up" with all the arrogant, manipulative, and self-centered university students. I'll never forget what he told me then.

"In my two years here, I've met more likable, well-adjusted, happy people than I did in all my time at the university. I want to spend the rest of my career with these people," as he pointed to the gyrating crowd of dancers. He and many of his co-workers genuinely enjoyed being with Wendy and his friends.

Since that time, Ralph and I have met dozens of people like this staff worker. Many of the female staff persons have called Wendy by affectionate names like "Sweetie," or "Handsome," or "Mister Flirt" and many male staffers have joined him outside to smoke and talk with him about cars and girls and family. Administrative staff personnel have always treated him with respect and affection as they have worked with him to improve his life.

For over 12 years he worked at a place that employs the disabled, a business called Pride Industries. Work consisted of folding towels, sorting cans and bottles for recycling, and packaging small items for shipping. As Wendy aged he was given the task of keeping the lunch room clean. A paycheck was issued every two weeks, W-2 forms were mailed each year and he was awarded "sick leave" and vacation pay. It was a regular job.

When he neared his 70th birthday, however, his supervisor called for an annual review session and asked me to attend. I learned then that my brother was "slowing down," and seemed more interested in going outside for a smoke or "catching a few winks" than he was in doing his job. That being said, his boss then announced, with eyes tearing up a bit,

"We love having Wendy here. There's no way in hell we would ever fire him. We're just wondering if there may be a place or a program that would be more satisfying for him. A place with less demand on him."

We were able to locate an adult day program run by the Easter Seal Foundation and available to Wendy, so arrangements were made for him to "retire" from Pride. We set up a system whereby he would receive $15 every week (a paycheck), designed to counter his main concern that he would not be "earning money" anymore if he moved. I checked with the manager at his new place several months after he started the new program to see how he was doing.

Her face brightened up as she told me, "Your brother is a 'sweetheart.' Every morning when I arrive, he's outside on his scooter waiting for me. He saves me a parking place and tells me to come in and have some coffee. We're so glad to have him here."

I thought of her and Eddie, and Mary, and Ryan, and David, and Rubio, and Carlos, and Dennis and Lucy and a host of others who have cared for my brother. Most of them, working for minimum wage or slightly higher, have demonstrated a compassion and tenderness for their charges that has far exceeded their job responsibilities. They are the sweethearts.

When I remember them and the affection they have shown to my brother, I think of what Jesus said–"If you have done it to the least of these, you have done it unto Me."

A CHILD FOREVER

On the occasions when I have attempted to describe my brother to people who haven't yet met him, I have struggled to find words that would help them picture what he is like. Some have had little or no experience with mentally-disabled persons. Others have known a few people with Down Syndrome, or Autism, or Cerebral Palsy. . .but they haven't met Wendy, who will probably be a new phenomenon to them. In these later years, describing him has become even more difficult because, on top of his disabilities, he is now a "little old man" who has no teeth, smokes cigarettes, and often wears a beard, mustache or goatee. He is "one-of-a-kind."

Invariably, when these new people fish for clues to know what he is like, and they will ask, "Well, what is his I.Q.?" I answer this question by replying, "Doctors have told us that he has the I.Q. of a 5-year old, but they really don't know (it is hard to measure I.Q. with someone who doesn't read). He's like a little child, trapped in an old man's body. Don't let his looks fool you."

Since giving out this characterization dozens of times, I am satisfied that this response is a pretty fair representation of Wendy. After spending a few minutes with him, newcomers soon begin to catch-on. He is a child <u>and</u> a man, with more child than man in him.

Both nature and environment have made him to be playful like a child. For years, Ralph and I have toyed with him in childish ways throughout his lifetime. Hundreds of times we have held up 4 fingers and then asked him,

"How many fingers do you see?"

He will say, "Four."

Bending one down, we will ask, "Now, how many?"

He will say "Three.

We will bend another. "How many?"

"Two."

And finally, we bend the third finger, leaving the universal symbol of disgust, "the finger." He will laugh and then grab at it yelling, "Wha, wha, wha, you cut out that crap!"

One of us will initiate a "memory test" by asking if he remembers Grandpa, Grandma, Aunt Dorothy and others. He will always answer, "Sure." Then we will ask if he remembers our sister Ruthie. Again, Wendy responds, "Sure."

When we tell him that we have never had a sister named Ruthie, Wendy will smile and say, "Wha, wha, wha, I'm know it."

We have playfully "tortured" him by stealing his cigarettes, hiding his money, squirting him with garden hoses, knocking off his hat and taking away his keys, but every time he sees what we're doing and laughs with us, enjoying every minute of it. When people have accused us of being "mean" to Wendy, we have to inform them that teasing has always been a way of life in the Jacobson home. After all, why would you call kids "kids" if they didn't kid?

Wendy is terribly afraid of water, so when we have access to a swimming pool, we naturally chide him into getting in the pool with us. He is so anxious to be included that he will comply. Big mistake! He is "at our mercy." I will float him in my arms as I ask him to repeat after me, "Knock, knock, who's there?"

He echoes my question, to which I respond, "John."

He knows to say, "J, J, J, John who?'

I say, "John the Baptist," as I dunk him under the water.

In spite of his hydrophobia, he always comes up laughing with delight. He will even want to do it again, only permitting <u>him</u> do the dunking. "Wha, wha, wha my turn."

Wendy's turn at "John the Baptist," circa 1961.

Whenever he comes for a sleep-over and it's time to go to bed, we conduct a regular bedtime ritual. I will help put on his "jammies," then throw him down on the bed and perform an old-fashioned "whisker-burn" on his tummy (a callback from our childhood years with Dad). He thrashes and squeals, "Wha, wha, you dirty rat!" Then he grabs me, rolls me over with his strong left hand and proceeds to return the favor. It is as if, in that moment, he becomes a little child again. We finish the game, say our prayers, he kisses me goodnight and drifts off in "la la land." He sleeps like a baby.

In addition to his playfulness, he embodies another central attribute of childhood—the world revolves around him. He is essentially self-centered. Though he is very aware of and sensitive to hurting people (as noted), some-how, any event or crisis will eventually work its way back to number one. For example, when my wife had been in a minor car accident and had a broken rib, I called Wendy to tell him about it. He was so distraught by the news that he immediately asked me if he could spend the night at my house because <u>he</u> was so "shook up." Never mind, that my wife was the one with injuries. He was worried and needed attention.

When tragedy strikes someone in his world, such as the death or divorce or illness, Wendy will demonstrate his sad-ness for a time, but then quickly move to priority concerns–his own needs. Just as a young mother is enabled to overcome hunger and sleep deprivation in service to her needy infant, we are often empowered to face our own loss by tending to our 70 year-old child.

Wendy's child-like qualities have often defined him. In many ways he has never grown up and will never do so, but this childishness is a big part of his charm and effect. During some of the most horrid times of my own adult life and the lives of my family members, these qualities have surfaced to raise us out of the "abyss". In somber times his playfulness has cheered us. In times of self-pity his insistence on "the now" has re-directed us. In shameful times his innocence has restored us. In times of discouragement his hopefulness has lifted us. Maybe what the prophets wrote is true for us, ". . .and they shall be led by a little child."

I realize that the day will come when Wendy will leave us, and the sadness of that day will be unbearable, but even greater than our sorrow will be the wonderful memories he has left behind. We will always remember how special he was to us. I hope that when he gets to heaven he won't be changed too much (maybe a little) because if he is too "normal," too adult we may not recognize him. Besides, I want him to be the man we have always known. . .a child forever.

JAKE AND NEVA

When one steps back and looks at Wendy's life, the way he has touched people's lives, his fortitude in the face of adversity, his unique spirit of love and kindness and his remarkable longevity, the question must come to mind, "How did he come to be like this?" I am sure that part of the answer is that it "took a village" of teachers, care-givers, church people, friends, and even two fairly decent brothers, but more than all of these is that fact that he had two great parents.

Dad was the only son among five daughters born to the Reverend and Mrs. A. H. Jacobson. By definition a P.K. (preacher's kid), he not only grew up living with the high expectations of his father's congregations to be a "cut above" the other children of his day, but also shouldered the burden of carrying-on the Jacobson family name. We do not know exactly how it all came about, but Dad revolted against these pressures and developed into a type of renegade; a "black sheep of the family." He began smoking cigarettes at an early age. He was known as a prankster and a joker. He often got in trouble, incurring public scorn and the wrath of his father.

In spite of all of his rebelliousness, people loved him. A few years ago while visiting some of his old friends in a nursing home in Lindsborg, Kansas, I discovered that Jake, as Dad was called, had won the affections of most of the people around him despite, and perhaps because of, his mischievousness and chicanery. In his late teen years he had left his home town to work with some migrant workers who moved across Kansas during wheat-harvesting season, and wound up in Oberlin, Kansas, where he met Neva Rydquist, destined to become our mother.

As children we knew nothing of his past life (most kids don't). All we knew was that he was our dad, that he lived with us, disciplined us, worked to provide for us and played with us. When we were growing up, we sensed that our friends enjoyed being with him as much as being with us. Adult friends streamed into our home to enjoy time with Mom and Dad. Without really noticing, we saw how he cared for people and loved all three of us equally, and though he loved playing all the sports with Ralph and me (baseball, basketball, ping pong, etc.), we never felt like we were favored over Wendy, who received as much attention, maybe more, than either of us.

It was because of Dad that Wendy always felt so secure. The hours spent in teaching him to ride a bicycle, the hours spent driving around the block with him after work, the hours spent taking him on shopping trips and outings, all added up in Wendy's mind to convey the deep-rooted sense that "I am a person of worth."

Mom's roots were similar to Dad's. She was the fourth daughter in the string of seven children. Years later she would complain, "I was the fourth girl, and who wants a fourth girl. Besides, after me came two boys who my parents claimed had 'hung the moon.'" From all reports, she was feisty, independent and strong-willed. She left her small farm town at the age of 17 to work as a nanny in Washington State. Only after her father wrote her a letter saying that Jake was coming back to Oberlin, did she came back home. When she did return, they fell in love, married and then moved to Lindsborg, where Dad bought a service station, and settled down for what turned out to be a wild ride on the train of "family life."

They were part of what is now called "The Greatest Generation." They had values and morals as strong as steel. In addition, Mom and Dad had compassion and love for other people and forged deep friendships wherever they went. Our home was a magnet for kids and families alike, and within this swirl of relationships, Wendy was always unashamedly and proudly included near the center of activity. It was in our home, that he learned to be comfortable and confident in the company of all types of people, to laugh and play with them, to converse with them, to enjoy them..

Both Mom and Dad had great senses of humor. They had the kind of "take" on things that helped themselves and others not take life too seriously. They could, and would laugh at themselves. Teasing was the "language of love" in our home, a way of taking the time to figure out what would make us all laugh, and an odd style of giving attention to each other. For example, on one occasion when Ralph and I had tripped Dad from behind causing him to fall, he got up and shouted, "Boys, that's a lack of disrespect!" Ralph and I caught the double negative, and started to laugh. Instead of becoming more enraged, Dad quickly admitted to his own gaffe, briefly joined in the laughter. . .and then he sent us to our room.

One time, after a little league game, I found myself in the men's room with Dad and a fellow-coach. After they had finished their business, Dad made for the door. "Jake aren't you going to wash your hands?" his cohort asked. My dad just smiled and said, "No, Al. I didn't pee on them," as he walked out confidently with a smirk of satisfaction.

Mom had a similar style of humor, one that would force sudden shifts in her listeners' thought processes. A few years ago, after our step-father, Herb had spent a night in the hospital and had returned to their home, he asked

Mom pleadingly, "Did you miss me?" Without blinking Mom replied, "Were you gone?" Herb did not seem phased by this because he had become accustomed to Mom's humor. He would often shower her with hyperbolic praise, such as, "I'm married to the most wonderful woman in the world. She would quickly retort, "Who's he talkin' about? Has Herb been drinkin' again (he didn't drink)?" With Ralph and me, she would often "pop our balloons" by saying, with a twinkle in her eye, things like, "We should have taken the money we spent on your education and given it to Wendy," or "If Wendy had been normal, he'd have given both of you a run for your money," or "Ralph, you drive like a yahoo!" or "Lyle, with all that education, why aren't you any smarter than you are?"

In her late-80s, as she slipped into old-age dementia, the decline could not dull her quick wit or her sense of humor. Ralph would take her in for periodic medical exams to evaluate the pace of her dementia. The doctor would ask a series of questions about the date, the time of day, her address, etc. to see how her memory was functioning. After a few answers, Mom would ask her own question, "Do they actually pay you money to ask these questions?" The doctors loved to have her come and when she was told that her memory was failing, she responded quickly, "There are a lot things I don't want to remember."

None of us boys can ever forget what our parents wove into the fabric of our lives, especially Wendy's. They laughed instead of frowning when he fell, or stammered, or used funny words to describe things. He watched these reactions and learned to laugh at his own foibles. He learned to move beyond his own limitations without embarrassment. They did not allow him to see himself as a burden to our family, but rather an asset, an important part of our lives. He learned to appreciate himself just as he was, and so, came to accept and appreciate the world around him.

Wendy is like he is, primarily because of Mom and Dad. Their parenting skills are even more vivid in the light of Wendy's limited capacity to process words or ideas. The admirable qualities fused into his life were transferred not by words or precepts but by their living. If young parents ever wonder what it is in their parenting that will have the most impact on their children, words or behavior, they should look at Wendy. He is the product of two parents living out their lives unpretentiously in the presence of one who could only learn how to live by what he saw and what he felt, not by what he understood with his mind.

Harry Chapin's classic song, "Cat's in the Cradle," could have been written to describe the impact of Mom and Dad on Wendell's life . . .their boy was just like them.

YOU LOOK LIKE YOUR BROTHER

Even though they say that "blood is thicker than water," the blood between some brothers is often not thick at all. For others it has actually turned into "bad blood." This is the reason why one expression for exasperation is "Oh brother!" For many siblings, having a brother or brothers is anything but pleasant. Times together feel more like duty or drudgery than delight, and are often soured by jealousy, resentment, criticism or competition. But when I think of Wendy, Ralph and myself, I realize that our blood has been much thicker than water and has shown itself to be stronger than Cerebral Palsy, stronger than age, or distance, or intelligence, or even social pressure. We have actually enjoyed being with each other (most of the time) and can look back over our lives with gratitude for the privilege of being brothers.

Mom and Dad imprinted on our minds and hearts that we possessed a special, unbreakable bond with each other. They diffused jealousy by showing us that we were of equal value in their eyes and eventually we came to see ourselves through this same lens. They would introduce us as their "three boys" with uniform pride, never flinch when speaking of Wendy, nor for that matter, gloat too much when referring to Ralph or me. We were a unit, "the Jacobson boys," "their three boys."

The fact that Wendy was handicapped did not diminish the level of companionship, but actually enhanced it in many ways. We included him in most of our childhood activities. He went to baseball practice with us and always got a turn to bat. We would applaud him when he finally made contact with the ball, and even though we teased (and occasionally mocked) him as he attempted to catch or throw, he loved being a part of our spring and summer sports obsessions. Beyond attending our games and cheering us on from the stands, he helped us fold newspapers for our paper routes, helped mow the lawn or change oil in the car. He was a full-fledged member of our gang. He was always close-by.

Mom and Dad drilled into our consciousness that we were to "take care" of our older brother, and though Ralph had come to assume the role of "big brother," both of us kept watchful eyes on him to make sure he was safe and happy. During our high school years, when peer pressures typically evoke embarrassment and timidity in the presence of fellow teenagers, Ralph drove Wendy and me unashamedly to school each day in his pink Ford convertible, so our friends grew to appreciate and enjoy this unique brother of ours. Our role in his life continued as he grew into adulthood, as both of us shared the responsibility of helping him adjust to new environments and navigate through the social services system. We have made sure that he was being treated well, and have provided little perks to make his life more enjoyable.

Life together was not always "peaches and cream" for us, however. Like all kids, we argued and fought occasionally. Our parents used even these times to reinforce the significance of our relationship by saying, "Stop hitting each other. You are brothers!" Our bickering sometimes escalated, and on one occasion, Mom reached the boiling point.

Ralph, Wendy and me, 2009.

"OK, you boys want to fight. I'm going to see to it that you have a good fight. Get out in the back yard!" she ordered, as she marched us outside with a belt in her hand. "Now start hitting each other!" Of course we'd lost our interest in fighting by the time we had reached the back door, but Mom was not fooled. Whack, went the belt. We started crying. Again, the belt struck at our legs until we resumed throwing punches at each other. I'm sure she would have been reported to Child Protective Services today, but her plan worked. We didn't fight for weeks. Of course, we never fought with Wendy. He was exempt. The closest thing to a fight for him was when we would trip him, roll him in the grass and tickle him until he squealed "Uncle."

Now during the senior years of our lives, the connection between us is stronger than ever. Wendy obsesses over having regular contact with us. He needs to know when we will be coming over to see him and he cannot go one day without talking to us on the phone. These daily conversations are annoyingly repetitive, but we answer or call because we know that he will not rest until he's made his call. If we have been with him during the day, we will sometimes tease him by saying, "Since we've had this time together, I guess you won't need to call tonight. Right?"

He will always respond the same way, "Wha, wha, wha I <u>call</u> you tonight. Wha, wha, wha, I'm checkin' up on you. Wha, me wan' talk to you in private."

If we have travel plans, he always needs to know where we are going, how we are getting there and when we are coming home. He will then ask us to bring back something for him from our trip. When Ralph returns home he always gets hit with the same question, "Wha, wha, wha you bring me something?" and he always gives the same response,

"I couldn't find anything good enough for you, Wendy" and then hands him a couple bucks (2 single dollar bills are better than 1 five).

Wendy's response is always the same. "Wha, wha, wha thank, thank, thank ver' much my big brother I love so much."

We occasionally try to test his allegiance to us by asking, "Who's your favorite brother? Ralph or me?" and sometimes will dangle a couple dollars in front of him to seduce a confession of favoritism. He never compromises. Never. His stock answer is "Wha, wha wha both!"

Wendy sees himself as part of both Ralph and me, and I suppose we see ourselves as part of him. His full name is Wendell Kent Jacobson, but often times when we come up he will become energized and excitedly say to us, "Wha, wha, my big brother, Mr. Ralph Kent Jacobson" or "Wha, wha, my big brother, Mr. Lyle Kent Jacobson." I don't think this is a result of confusion in his stunted mind, but rather an awareness of something deeper. We are in the middle of his life. He sees himself in us.

About 8 or 9 years ago, I went after work to pick up Wendy at The Garden to take him on a little outing in my truck. When I didn't see him smoking out on his patio as he usually was, I went inside to ask where I could find him. Manning the front desk was a young Hispanic staff member whom I did not recognize from my previous visits. I said to him, "I'm Wendell Jacobson's brother. Can you tell me where he is?"

He looked at me for just a split second and then replied in broken English, "Oh, yes, he down in the snack room." Then he added, "I can tell you are Wendell's brother. . .you look like him."

I was stunned by his comment. I flinched with embarrassment as I pictured Wendy's wrinkled, sunken, whiskered face, his unconcerned toothless lip protruding out beyond his chin, his bent, twisted posture. I had been told that my looks were close-to, even maybe a notch above average, so when I heard that I looked like Wendy, my ego began to tremble under the force of this comparison. I smiled at the attendant, seemingly satisfied by his astute observation and simply responded with, "Thank you very much."

As I walked away from the desk toward the snack room, I realized that in the nano-second it took for this young man to look into my face, he had seen something in me that he had seen in Wendy, qualities that went beyond our looks, perhaps something in our spirits that hinted of our common bond. After composing myself a bit, I quietly became grateful that someone had seen beyond our superficial differences. He had seen that Wendy and I were, at the core. . .brothers.

EPILOGUE

On June 25, 2011, just after I had completed writing my account of Wendy's life, he celebrated his 71st birthday. All the "usual suspects" were present–his brothers and "second mother," his extended family, long-term friends, several neighbors, his day program manager and staffers who had cared for him 8 to10 years prior. Many of the themes of his life and personality played out on this single day.

He drove his scooter over to my house a couple hours early so he would have time to ingest a few cigawrecks before the guests arrived. As friends and family drifted in he quizzed them on which car they had driven to the party, and if they owned a second vehicle, he inquired as to where they had left their other car. One guest had come in a new pick-up truck, which prompted Wendy to check it out by taking a short drive around the block.

A young couple from his apartment complex came to the party. Since I had never met them, I asked how they had come to know my brother. "Well, on the day we moved-in, Wendy drove up in his scooter and asked if we needed any help." Evidently they were touched by his friendliness and enamored by his uniqueness so they began inviting him over for afternoon chats and regular trips to Starbucks for coffee.

Former staff members, who had worked with Wendy at The Garden, sat around after gifts had been opened to recount experiences they had had during their years with him. They remembered Rosie, Wendy's passion for his scooter and funny things he had said or done. The manager at his current day program had driven across town to get to the party, and reported on how much everybody at the Easter Seal center enjoyed Wendy. She told me later, "He's one of the sweetest men I've ever met."

Even before everyone had dispersed, Wendy announced that his birthday would be on a Monday next year and that everyone was invited to come to his party. Shortly after the party he began reminding me and Diann about the "State Fair Overnight" in August and his trip to Oroville in April of next year.

When I told a number of the guests that I had been writing a book about Wendy, entitled "Good Lookin' Man Like Me," my son-in-law asked me how I had come up with that title. I told him that the phrase is one of Wendy's stock one-liners he uses to describe himself and that it capsulizes his positive spin on life. Mark had never heard Wendy use the phrase. Later that evening, while having dinner with the family, Wendy began to repeat his announcement about his upcoming birthday next year, and as if on cue, he turned to Mark and said, "You, you, you, you better come my birthday party next year, see good lookin' man like me. Wha, I be waitin' for you 'round corner."

Upon reviewing this one day and reflecting on the many years of Wendy's life, I was again filled gratitude for having him as my brother. Throughout all the turbulence of my personal life, he has been a steady and predictable source of stability. He has accommodated many of my bad choices and relished many of my good choices. My irritation over his quirks is often stilled by his stubborn love and constant affirmation of me and the people I love. The pain of our mutual sorrows and disappointments has been softened many times by his simple focus on the good things that remain. At times when I have resented difficulties in my own life, his stamina in the face of unimaginable handicaps has inspired me to "buck up" and move on past my pitiful, petty problems.

I have come to realize how blessed I have been to share a life with a good lookin' man like him.

www.ingramcontent.com/pod-product-compliance
Lightning Source LLC
Chambersburg PA
CBHW070107070426
42448CB00038B/1838